TRANSLATING EVALUATION INTO POLICY

Volume 3
SAGE RESEARCH PROGRESS SERIES IN EVALUATION

SAGE RESEARCH PROGRESS SERIES IN EVALUATION

General Editor: SUSAN E. SALASIN, *National Institute of Mental Health*
Co-Editor (1979): ROBERT PERLOFF, *University of Pittsburgh*

EDITORIAL REVIEW BOARD

SAGE RESEARCH PROGRESS SERIES IN EVALUATION
Volume 3

Edited by
ROBERT F. RICH

TRANSLATING EVALUATION INTO POLICY

Published in cooperation with the
EVALUATION RESEARCH SOCIETY

SAGE PUBLICATIONS   Beverly Hills   London

For information address:

SAGE Publications, Inc.
275 South Beverly Drive
Beverly Hills, California 90212

SAGE Publications Ltd
28 Banner Street
London EC1Y 8QE, England

Printed in the United States of America

Library of Congress Cataloging in Publication Data
Main entry under title:

Translating evaluation into policy.

   (Sage research progress series in evaluation; v. 3)
   Bibliography: p.
   1. Evaluation research (Social action programs)
2. Policy sciences. I. Rich, Robert F. II. Series.
H62.T63   309   79-21453
ISBN 0-8039-1283-8
ISBN 0-8039-1284-6 pbl

FIRST PRINTING

Contents

ABOUT THIS SERIES

The SAGE RESEARCH PROGRESS SERIES IN EVALUATION is a series of concisely edited works designed to present notable, previously unpublished writing on topics of current concern to the evaluation community. In keeping with a vision of evaluation as a methodological enterprise with outcomes at both the policy-making and services delivery levels, the series is designed to present state-of-the-art volumes for use by instructors and students of evaluation, researchers, practitioners, policy-makers, and program administrators.

Each volume (4 to 6 new titles will be published in each calendar year) focuses on themes which emerge from the previous year's annual meeting of the Evaluation Research Society—revised and supplemented by specially commissioned works.

The series begins in 1979 with five volumes, largely selected from papers delivered at the 2nd Annual Meeting of the Evaluation Research Society held in Washington, D.C. on November 2-4, 1978. The volumes in this inaugural year include:

QUALITATIVE AND QUANTITATIVE METHODS IN EVALUATION RESEARCH, edited by Thomas D. Cook and Charles S. Reichardt

EVALUATOR INTERVENTIONS: Pros and Cons, edited by Robert Perloff

TRANSLATING EVALUATION INTO POLICY, edited by Robert F. Rich

THE EVALUATOR AND MANAGEMENT, edited by Herbert C. Schulberg and Jeanette M. Jerrell

EVALUATION IN LEGISLATION, edited by Franklin M. Zweig

We are pleased that these initial volumes in the *SAGE RESEARCH PROGRESS SERIES IN EVALUATION* so well represent significant interdisciplinary contributions to the literature. Comments and suggestions from our readers will be welcomed.

SERIES EDITORS:

Susan E. Salasin, National Institute of Mental Health
Robert Perloff, University of Pittsburgh

EDITOR'S
INTRODUCTION

Evaluation researchers have long felt that their work *can* and *should* have a direct impact on program decision-making. Indeed, some researchers have proclaimed that "utilization would probably be most widely accepted as the single most important criteria of the success of evaluation research" (Cook, 1978). Authors cannot always agree on what is meant by "evaluation," but they do agree on the fact that in a democratic decision-making system, research designed to assess the impacts of programs should have a role in policy discussions. The extent and nature of this role is often debated among the academic and policy-making communities.

However, there is very little disagreement over (1) the belief that social science research (and evaluation research in particular) should have a substantial or very large effect on the formulation of national policy (Staats, 1979)—a recent survey revealed that 70 percent of top management officials in federal agencies agreed with this statement (Staats, 1979)—and (2) neither policy makers nor academicians are satisfied with the "current state of the art" in translating research results into usable products or into techniques for problem-solving. As Patton (1978) reports, most of the recent literature is unanimous in announcing the general failure of evaluation research to affect decision-making in a significant way.

Policy makers and researchers often differ over their explanations for the gap between the perceived need to use research results and the apparent ability to translate this "need" into "practice." Recent thinking about this gap has been shaped by the "two-communities theory" (Dunn, forthcoming; Caplan, 1979). It is presumed that communication blockages, concerns over the quality of information, the nature of the decision-making process and the constraints the process places on utilization, and concerns over timeliness of the information account for "serious underutilization" of knowledge (Rich, forthcoming). The two-

7

communities theory attempts to identify the factors affecting utilization in terms of the *overall cultural experience* of the user (Dunn, forthcoming). One may have to understand the attitudes, background, reward system, and problem-solving style of each culture before one can come to definitive conclusions.

THE ROLE OF EVALUATION RESEARCH

Evaluation research represents a special case of assessing the role of social science research in the policy-making and implementation process. As Aaron (1978: 164) points out, we are reaching a point where

one can dismiss both the scorn of analysts for policy makers who do not act promptly on the latest findings and the scorn of policy makers for analysts whose every pen stroke does not inform tomorrow morning's decisions.

The two-communities perspective has something to offer those interested in explaining why utilization does not occur. However, the trend is clear: Social science research on the formulation of social and economic policy-making is likely to continue to increase.

Academicians and policy makers need to become concerned with finding alternative ways for fitting analysis (evaluation) into a broader perspective. The social sciences, in general, have succeeded in having their perspective adopted as part of regular government practice: Programs should be evaluated in terms of their demonstrable effects (Aaron, 1978). Evaluation research, however, should not be looked to for instrumental needs—as the sole basis on which to make specific decisions (Rich and Zaltman, 1978; Weiss, 1978). As Stokes (1978) has noted: "If program evaluations are felt by agency officials to be directed only to ultimate questions of whether a program should live or die, the benefits for program planning that much evaluation research provides will be lost." Government officials (and academicians) should learn to expect different kinds of returns from varied investments in knowledge production and application. It would be a mistake to apply the same tests of relevance and utility to knowledge which was designed (1) to increase our understanding of a problem or give us a different perspective on a problem and (2) for purposes of forming and/or implementing policy. One also adheres to a parochial view when it is assumed that empirical knowledge is the only valid type of information that should influence policy-making.

Seen as a whole, obstacles to and potentials for more useful social science and research pose profound questions about man as a problem solver, about knowledge
and craft, about science, and about a complex social and political order in which
knowledge and science are embedded and are shaped [Lindblom and Cohen,
1979: 3].

We need to understand program evaluation as a part of social problem-
solving. Thus, the task before us is not to formulate a single strategy
which would be designed to ensure "utilization success"; instead, we
need to identify a few variables which might make a difference in a
significant number of evaluation cases (Weiss, 1972).

This volume is designed to suggest what some of these variables might
be in different policy areas. The contribution of this collection of essays
does not lie in identifying many new perspectives on utilization; instead,
it offers the perspective of practitioners at the national and state levels
on how to perform utilization-oriented evaluations.

EVALUATION RESEARCH AS PROBLEM-SOLVING

Evaluation research can be understood only as part of an overall
political process (Weiss, 1975). The political process should be understood as a problem-solving process: problems are identified, defined,
and "grappled with." "Problem-solving" is often thought of as a process
which results in an outcome that by some standard represents an improvement over the previously existing situation (Lindblom and Cohen,
1979).

In this literature, "solving" a problem does not require an understanding of the issues involved; it only requires reaching an outcome
that is considered to be acceptable by all "stake-holders."

It is important to realize that this "outcome" may not represent a
long-term solution of any problem—it may simply represent a compromise that is acceptable at a given point in time. People may also feel
coerced into accepting a particular outcome. In Lindblom and Cohen's
terms, there may not be any improvement over the previously existing
situation. "Solution," therefore, would seem to be a misnomer. "Problem grappling" seems to reflect the process that individuals and political
institutions go through in reaching a particular outcome.

As Lindblom (1978), Simon (1948), Levine (1972), Janis and Mann
(1977), and Braybrook and Lindblom (1963) have suggested, "coordination of complexity" is an important way in which one might think about

"problem-grappling." The problem of coordination is one of the key concerns of modern managers—organizational coordination internally as well as externally.

It follows from this literature that successful managers can be characterized as those who successfully gain control over the organization or suborganization for which they are responsible. In order to gain control, the managers will *assemble* whatever resources are necessary to achieve this goal; furthermore, the resources will be *maintained* because the process of retaining control is a continual problem—not because of devious or immoral challenges, but simply because of increased complexity, specialization, and growth. This process of gaining and retaining control has been identified as part of the political environment in which evaluation research must operate.

Problem-Solving Activities and Styles

WHAT DO WE MEAN BY PROBLEM-SOLVING?

Beyond being responsible for coordination and control, managers are held responsible for the "success of the organization." Success may be expressed in terms of power, profits, innovativeness, quality of service delivered, number of people served, and other measures designed to indicate the progress made by the organization in realizing its mission. Generally, the progress toward reaching these goals may be classified as the "problem-solving process"—the process of getting from here to there while overcoming obstacles and resistances. It is critical to remember that we are dealing with a process—problems seldom get solved, and it is probably misleading to believe that they do, or to orient programs toward the goal of reaching a solution. Rather, one makes progress toward goals. Goals may be adjusted and readjusted over time to take into account past developments.

PROBLEM-SOLVING ACTIVITIES

In making progress toward individual or organizational goals of managers, it is generally the case that certain generic types of activities are engaged in:

(1) *Problem definition:* the process of eliciting multiple definitions of a social problem and selecting the definition or set of definitions which appear most appropriate and specifying the structure of the problem—that is, the forces or variables inherent in the problem.

(2) *Clients identification:* (a) determining who the individual, informal groups, or formal organizations are who are the intended beneficiaries (primary clients) of the program; (b) determining who the individual, informal groups, or formal organizations are who in some way affect the impact of a program on an unintended beneficiary and who are thus secondary beneficiaries.

(3) *Specification of objectives:* specification of desired end-states for clients and/or managers as a result of a successful program.

(4) *Selection of general strategies:* determining what the relative use of facilitative, educative, persuasive, and power or coercive approaches should be in securing stated objectives.

(5) *Selection of tactics:* determining what specific activities a manager should undertake to encourage or require the acceptance of objectives by potential clients.

(6) *Implementation:* the process of interacting with clients through programmatic activities intended to encourage the adoption of specified objectives.

(7) *Evaluation:* the process of assessing whether or not desired or undesired outcomes have been reached, of specifying or explaining the outcomes that were reached, and of suggesting new strategies and/or definitions of future problems.

THE ROLE OF PROBLEM DEFINITION

In terms of analyzing the problem-solving process, we feel it is particularly important to look at the role of problem definition in "setting the stage" for or even controlling the policy-making process. Problem definitions are based on assumptions about the "causes" of a problem and where those causes lie. Studies have shown that the way a problem is defined *determines* the attempts at remediation, suggesting both the foci and techniques of intervention and by ruling out alternative possibilities (Caplan and Nelson, 1973). More specifically, problem definitions determine the strategy that is adopted to bring about change in a particular issue area (Mitroff and Mason, forthcoming; Mitroff and Kilman, 1978; Rich, 1979a).

By accepting the notion of competing sets of problem definitions, one stipulates that the problem-solving process has several different dimensions: scientific, political, social, and ethical/moral. Each of these dimensions is taken into account as a decision is being considered in various political areas.

PROBLEM—SOLVING STYLES

The way in which problem-solving activities are approached may be influenced by the style of the individual manager. It may be useful to think of problem-solving style as being a function of:

(a) *Background and training.*—In what field was an individual educated: What was the highest degree received?

(b) *Management experience.*—How long have persons been in their present positions, and what other types of management positions have they held?

(c) *Cognitive orientation toward information processing.*—Given that there is no rigid structure to the management process, it is particularly important to keep in mind the amount of discretion left to decision makers and human factors that play a role in influencing decisions. The informal or psychological guides used in information-processing are very important because they may result in: (1) restricting an individual's ability to gain new insights in problem-solving and (2) at the same time limiting the individual's ability to recognize that preconceptions are not supported by evidence—particularly with respect to empirically grounded data and outside expertise.

(d) *Information-processing ideology.*—It is well established that managers seek to avoid risk—official actions should be subject to the least possible risk. Organizations are likely to resist new sources and types of information, especially when they bring "bad news" and "turbulence."

The literature makes it clear that "experts" have a definite bias against information they find potentially threatening, and information which is not consistent with their core of values. If managers are not relying on their own knowledge or judgment, it is critical that the risk taken in using this alternative source of information is calculable. Thus, it is not surprising that managers seek to control the sources of information available to them (Rich, 1979a).

Given this background, one should compare and contrast the strategies of academicians searching for information with those of managers making such a search. Both the academician and the manager attempt to minimize *cost* and *risk*. They may, however, operationalize these terms quite differently.

The Academic Perspective

One should understand what is meant by *risk avoidance* within an organizational context. When scientists or academicians are faced with a problem, they continue to search for new information (from any possible source) until they feel "comfortable" that the solution they have come up with cannot be negated at "this point in time." Scientists welcome new information (if it is received at zero cost or at minimum cost) to test their probable solutions against the null hypothesis. Once the results are made public, other scientists are invited to continue testing for a new solution or for refinement of the original solution. In this case, risk reduction is directly related to the "search for truth"; cost can be defined in time (especially trade-offs with these activities) and in real monetary terms.

The Manager's Perspective

In a political environment (such as bureaucracy) risk avoidance or reduction has taken on a different meaning. When officials or managers first receive new information, they ask: "Why am I receiving this information? What does the sender want from me?" If these questions can be answered to managers' satisfaction, they are then likely to inquire: "If I use this information, can I be embarrassed?" Embarrassment may consist of: (a) presentation of more up-to-date information by an official from another organization at a meeting; (b) presentation of information which contradicts the program most favored by top management; (c) presentation of information which others are already familiar with; or (d) presentation of information which puts another organization into a more favorable light than the one represented by the manager. The concepts of cost and risk are clearly related to the realities of politics. In an environment in which competition for scarce resources is intense, officials do not want to make a mistake (Rich, 1979a).

THE ROLE OF EVALUATION

Within the context of minimizing risk, it is crucial to understand the role of evaluation in the overall problem-solving process. As individuals are constantly in the position of accepting or rejecting ideas and/or strategies for changes that are proposed, one might hypothesize that we have implicit evaluation models which are used to guide our individual decision-making processes.

Evaluation is not only a stage in the problem-solving process, but it also represents the time at which one moves from formulating and implementing ideas/programs (the action phase) to the point of assessing/judging what the success of this program was and whether it should be continued in the future.

Evaluation researchers have attempted to systematize this process of assessment into a formal research methodology. Public officials were being asked to replace their implicit, well-learned models with a new, unproven mode of inquiry. This formal model of inquiry was steeped in scientific tradition and legitimated by well-known and respected practitioners of that tradition. Policy makers were uncomfortable with this new tool of research—it was not as reliable (and perhaps not even as valid) as intuition or experience.

Despite these reservations, evaluation research has matured into a discipline and is recognized by both academicians and practitioners as an important part of the problem-solving process. With Congress' increasing emphasis on accountability (for example, Sunset legislation) and oversight, one can expect the overall federal budget devoted to evaluation to increase.

In terms of evaluating the role that research can/should play in decision-making, it should be remembered that not all decision-making situations lend themselves to the full and open use of evaluation research. For example, when managers are engaged in negotiations, research probably will not be the critical input in the decision-making process. Indeed, managers need to consider the goals or objectives of the organization and the options that are available that will help in reaching these goals. To try to orient an information system to fit into this process is probably futile. If it is done, one should not be surprised to find that the information system is not being applied. This analysis is equally true for constituency-building (although some public opinion data might be useful) and parts of almost every other activity. Again, one must remember that the research process is indeed different from the management/political process: There are different stakes and constituencies involved. More importantly, there are different standards which apply to what constitutes a successful outcome. Janis (1977) would characterize as a successful outcome one that was scientifically rational. Most managers would characterize it as one which met the goals of the organization, minimized costs, and brought maximum gain to the organization—they had to give up very few "blue chips." *The two outcomes need not be the same.*

THE VALUE OF TRANSLATING EVALUATION INTO POLICY

In assessing the role of evaluation research in policy-making, it has already been noted that one should not expect to use all evaluation results in the same way; similarly, Congress should not fund all evaluation research with the same objective in mind (Stokes, 1978). In this context, it is also worth noting that not all evaluation research is necessarily valuable; one should not make the assumption that because research is available, it should necessarily be used. Other modes of problem-solving (tossing a coin or voting) may be far superior to the application of empirical knowledge (Lindblom and Cohen, 1979).

Similarly, if change is brought about through the adoption of evaluation research, one should not necessarily assume that it is valuable. The

unintended consequences or yields from change may be the most important and pervasive. Clearly, it is fair to say that change for change's sake
is not something to be valued. One should be oriented toward asking
questions about what, for whom, and under what conditions change is
valuable.

The change literature definitely has a rationalistic bias in its analyses
and discussions of value. Public officials often confuse what is valuable
to themselves with what is valuable to the client—what is of value to a
public official may not contribute to the well-being of a client. For
example, the fact that a community mental health center serves many
people (many people are coming to the center), that it increases its
budget by attracting third-party payments, and that it gains recognition
through public relations does not necessarily mean that the community
is being well served. It is easy to assume that status, prestige, and funding
are equitable with the value of high-quality services as measured by low
rates of recidivism and high scores on level-of-functioning measures by
clients. One should, therefore, distinguish between "valuable change"
and "change" (Rich and Zaltman, 1978).

CONTRIBUTIONS TO THIS VOLUME

This volume makes a significant contribution to the discussion of
translating evaluation research results into policy in several different
respects:

(1) It offers practitioners perspective on how evaluation research has and should be
    used in public policy settings (Woy, Waizer, Neigher, Morss). These perspectives
    are offered in different policy areas and at different levels of government—ranging
    from state and local government to evaluation's role in international relations.
(2) It presents frameworks for thinking about evaluation, problem-solving, and public
    policy-making (Delbecq and Gill, and Radnor).
(3) New original empirical research on the relationship between evaluation and
    policy-making is presented (Windle et al., Rich, and Morss).

Given these different perspectives, the book will be interesting to
those who want to compare the role of evaluation in different policy
areas, at different levels of government from the perspective of both
practitioners and academicians.

Practitioner Perspectives

Woy, Waizer, and Neigher examine the role of evaluation research in decision-making related to mental health. Each of these individuals is currently employed as a practitioner at federal, state, and/or community levels. Radnor offers the perspective of a researcher who has assessed the role of evaluation from the law enforcement perspective (LEAA). Woy examines program evaluation in relation to two nationally supported community mental health programs: the Community Mental Health Centers (CMHC) Program and the Community Support Program (CSP). Since 1969, the National Institute for Mental Health (NIMH) has conducted over 50 evaluations of the CMHC Program at a cost of approximately $5 million. To date, there are no complete evaluations of the CPS Program. Nevertheless, there are lessons to be learned from both programs. Woy focuses on these lessons as the major point of his essay. He identifies problem definition, the maintenance of data systems, and the need for careful planning as the key lessons to be learned. He is able to draw on concrete examples/experiences to illustrate why these points are particulary important.

Waizer reports on the role of evaluation for the CSP Program in New Jersey. He is particularly concerned with the impact of evaluation research on the state agency (Division of Mental Health and Hospitals) for which he works, and concludes that evaluation research has a major influence on policy-making in the state of New Jersey. Waizer points out that the close partnership of program evaluation staff with key decision makers accounts for the "successful utilization of the research." He also identifies the strong commitment of the division to the implementation of the CPS program goals as being important in accounting for relatively high levels of utilization.

Neigher, a director of a local CMHC, examines the same set of problems from the perspective of a local agency. Drawing on his experience (for data) and the literature on utilization (for a framework), Neigher concludes that there are several factors essential for maximizing utilization of evaluation research results: (a) a personal factor—someone takes responsibility for getting information to the right people; (b) a set of political factors—because evaluation operates in a political environment one should not always expect evaluation results to be used; and (c) a problem-solving factor—evaluation research is often used, but not in the manner in which we would like it to be used. Neigher strongly argues that evaluators should take steps toward creating *realistic, a priori* expectations about the craft of evaluation and its usefulness.

From the perspective of aid to developing countries and the importance of evaluation research, Morss offers a different set of perspectives. He points out that evaluation systems should track inputs and outputs against schedules, measure project effects, identify current and upcoming problems, diagnose reasons for problems, and prescribe project solutions. These are the same goals that evaluation research has in most policy settings.

Morss then goes on to point out why this desirable type of information system is not being employed in the project development context: (a) it represents a threat to management; (b) management is not able to anticipate information needs; (c) current methods of evaluation are extraordinarily costly; (d) relevant data are too expensive; (e) recommendations are offered which cannot be used; and (f) research designs are used which do not reflect the realities of the operating environment. The essay then provides some of the same recommendations offered by Neigher and other contributors.

Frameworks

Given these perspectives on utilization and policy-making, it is important to have an appropriate framework in which to organize these findings. The essays by Radnor, Delbecq and Gill, and Rich point to the importance of the problem-solving framework discussed earlier in this essay. Windle and his colleagues provide a different framework for thinking about the problem. This latter perspective is organized around different types and objectives of evaluation research.

Delbecq and Gill believe that utilization of research results is constrained by poor problem diagnosis, inappropriate patterns of interaction among groups, and what they call "bounded irrationality." Political actors' perspectives come in conflict with each other (That is, they are not able to resolve the conflict among competing assumptions), and inaction follows. It is the purpose of this essay to suggest a strategy for mediation among the competing perspectives.

Radnor and Hofler also identify the need to understand the overall problem-solving process. They suggest that a critical and neglected function of evaluation research is to aid in the process of organizational learning. In their view, evaluators have an inward-oriented focus which limits them to a single program and focuses their attention on the program per se. On the other hand, an outward-oriented evaluation focuses beyond the program itself to the context in which the program is embedded. In this case, evaluation research would be concerned both with the external environment in which the program is implemented and with the internal context of the agency which has developed the program. The authors suggest that both types of evaluation are important; the latter, in their view, has been neglected by evaluators and policy makers alike. By analyzing their experiences with the Law Enforcement Assistance Administration, Radnor and Hofler demonstrate how both types of evaluation can work.

Empirical Results

Finally, Windle and Rich offer empirical results from studies designed to assess the effectiveness with which evaluation is translated into policy. Windle assesses the NIMH experience in promoting the use of evaluation; Rich examines the area of unemployment insurance policy.

The Windle study is derived from a mail questionnaire to 181 community mental health centers in 1973. It also employs the results of a Philadelphia Health Management Corporation study. In the 1973 study, 24 different types of evaluation activities were identified across the 181 centers. Different types of evaluation were associated with greater and lesser levels of impact (that is, affect on the decision-making process). Windle concludes that in studying the impact of evaluation efforts on program changes, the issue of relations between program echelons (levels) becomes especially important.

The Rich study focuses on the contribution of evaluation research to problem-solving in the unemployment insurance area. In-depth interviews were completed with each of the major public officials (at the federal level) who spent a significant amount of their time working on this policy area. The study showed that it is essential to distinguish between formal and informal kinds of utilization.

CONCLUSIONS

Taken together, the essays in this volume offer a different perspective on the issues and problems associated with translating evaluation into policy. Many of the authors feel that insufficient attention is given to the natue of the problem-solving process. Each offers some strategies for increasing the quality and quantity of utilization.

It also seems clear that these authors are encouraging academicians and policy makers to distinguish between various types of knowledge.

Not all evaluation research utilization should be thought of from the same perspective. By making these types of distinctions, the reader will influence the investments that are made in evaluation research and the expectations that individuals have with respect to utilization.

—*Robert F. Rich*
Princeton University

REFERENCES

AARON, H. J. (1978) Politics and The Professors. Washington, DC: Brookings.

BRAYBROOK, D. and C. E. LINDBLOM (1963) A Strategy for Decision. New York: Free Press.

BELL, D. (1974) The Coming of Post-Industrial Society, New York: Basic Books.

CAPLAN, N. and S. D. NELSON (1973) "On being useful: The nature and consequences of psychological research on social problems." American Psychologist 28:199-211.

——— (1979) "The two communities theory and knowledge utilization." American Behavioral Scientist 22:459-470.

CAPLAN, A. MORRISON, R. J. STAMBAUGH (1975) The Use of Social Science Knowledge in Policy Decisions at the National Level: A Report to Respondents. Ann Arbor: Institute for Social Research, University of Michigan.

CAPLAN, N. and R. F. RICH (1976) "Open and closed knowledge inquiry systems: The process and consequences of bureaucratization of information policy at the national level." Presented at the meeting of the OECD conference on dissemination of economic and social development research results, Bogota, Colombia, June.

COOK, T. D. (1978) Evaluation Studies Review Annual (Vol. 3). Beverly Hills, CA: Sage.

DUNN, W. (forthcoming) "The two communities metaphor and model of knowledge use: An exploratory case survey." Knowledge 1.

JANIS, I. L. and L. MANN (1977) Decision-Making. New York: Free Press.

LEVINE, R. (1972) Public Planning: Failure and Redirection. New York: Basic Books.

LINDBLOM, C. (1978) Politics and Markets. New York: Basic Books.

——— and D. COHEN (1979) Usable Knowledge. New Haven, CT: Yale University Press.

MITROFF, I. and R. O. MASON (forthcoming) "A logic of strategic problem solving: A program of research and planning." Administrative Science Quarterly.

MITROFF, I. and R. H. KILMAN (1978) Methodological Approaches to Social Sciences. San Francisco: Jossey-Bass.

MORSS, E. and R. F. RICH (forthcoming) Government Information Management. Boulder, CO: Westview Press.

PATTON, M. Q. (1978) Utilization Focused Evaluation. Beverly Hills, CA: Sage.

RICH, R. F. (1979a) "Editor's introduction." American Behavioral Scientist 22:327-337.

——— (1979b) "Systems of analysis, technology assessment, and bureaucratic power." American Behavioral Scientist 22:393-416.

——— (forthcoming) The Power of Social Science Information and Public Policy-Making: The Case of the Continuous National Survey. San Francisco: Jossey-Bass.

—— and G. ZALTMAN (1978) "Toward a theory of planned social change: Alternative perspectives and ideas." Evaluation and Change (Special Issue):41-47.

SIMON, H. (1948) Administrative Behavior. New York: Macmillan.

STAATS, E. B. (1979) "Why isn't policy research utilized more by decision-makers?" Presented at the Annual Meeting of the Council of Applied Social Research, Annapolis, Maryland, June.

STOKES, D. E. (1978) Congressional Testimony Before the U.S. Senate Committee on Human Resources, October 6 and 27.

WEISS, C. H. [ed.] (1978) "Using social research in public policy making." Lexington, MA: D. C. Heath.

—— (1975) "Evaluation research in the political context." In E. Guttentag and E. L. Struening (eds.) Handbook of Evaluation Research (Vol. 1). Beverly Hills, CA: Sage.

—— (1972) Evaluation Research: Methods of Assessing Program Effectiveness. Englewood Cliffs, NJ: Prentice-Hall.

PART I
Policy-Making and Program Evaluation
General Models and Approaches

1

André L. Delbecq
University of Santa Clara

Sandra L. Gill
University of Wisconsin, Madison

POLITICAL DECISION-MAKING AND PROGRAM MOVEMENT

The recent rise of tax reform and increasing demands for accountability and effectiveness among human services have forcibly thrust the applied social sciences fully into the political arena. The need to bridge traditional gaps among applied scientists, human service professionals, and political decision makers has become critical for the months and years ahead.

To date, however, the diverse literatures dealing with policy-making, planning, program management, and evaluation offer few synthetic clues. Each remains segmented, with scholarly attention focused on theories, models, issues, and methodologies particular to a single domain (Cunningham, 1977: 463).

This separation in the academic realm is further exacerbated within the service delivery networks by segmentation of professional roles. Policy makers, planners, program implementors, and evaluators are common specialists. But the lament for their interaction and interrelationships during decision making (Weiss, 1977: 5-7) is obstructed by preferences for favored professional strategies and outcomes, largely the result of socialization within separate professional training programs. Roles enacted by such individuals emanate from different professional training programs and respond to different reward structures.

It is proposed in this chapter that each role set is likely to operate from different logics. Therefore, to advance "rationality"

23

in decision making, we propose that these actors will need to be increasingly familiar with their colleagues' professional values and utilities and will need to be sufficiently skilled in a repertoire of group decision making processes to negotiate between their differentiated logics. As Caplan (1977) suggests:

> The major problems that hamper utilization are nontechnical—that is, the level of knowledge utilization is not so much the result of a slow flow of relevant and valid knowledge from knowledge producers to policymakers, but is due more to factors involving values, ideology, and decision-making styles. Thus increased production of objective and policy relevant data or further development and improvements in knowledge storage and retrieval systems are unlikely to advance utilization unless accompanied by success in . . . bridg[ing] social science and policymaker perspectives [1977: 195-196].

Our purpose in this chapter is to present a heuristic paradigm built on decision variables, rules, and types to explain some origins of the discontinuity of rationality in political decision making. The paradigm is focused on four sets of functionally interrelated actors, policy makers, program administrators/implementors, and planners and evaluators; it also suggests (1) diagnostic clues regarding their individual decision making contexts and (2) complementary strategies and group processes which facilitate the integration of their decisions and efforts, ultimately enhancing the likelihood of "bounded rationality" (Simon, 1957).

DECISION VARIABLES FROM THE PERSPECTIVE OF POLICY MAKERS AND PROGRAM ADMINISTRATORS

Program development—that is, the composite of policy making, planning, service delivery, and evaluation—may be seen as the outcome of three essential decision components: (1) problem stimulus, (2) goal agreement, and (3) solution agreement. Our first proposition is that *throughout the drama of program development, each actor—policy maker, planner, pro-*

gram implementor, and evaluator—tends to respond to these three decision elements from a different perceptual "set" or basis, which leads to interactor variance in terms of preferred solution strategies or outcomes.

Problem Stimulus

All decision makers act from a stimulus—that is, perception of a problem. Nonetheless, even with respect to this first decision component of program development, there is cleavage among roles. For the policy maker the most important aspect is the political magnitude of expressed *demand* (Anderson, 1975: 15-18; Rakoff and Schaefer, 1970: 63). "Politicians are inclined to respond positively not to group needs but to group demands" (Parenti, 1974: 16). By contrast, the critical element for the program administrator or implementor is the perception of *need* which provides a raison d'être for enlarging organizational domain and increasing resource allocation (Mintzberg, 1976: 252, Pfeffer et al., 1976: 227). Thus, the motivating source of tension leading to problem perception differs.

For purposes of our model, this variable will be called "*Scale,*" simply implying the perceived number of people affected by a social condition, neutralizing, for the moment, the dichotomy between demand versus need.

Goal Agreement

For the program administrator, goal agreement is largely a function of congruence between professional practices and traditions, commonly expressed through organizational philosophy or agency goals where professionals are allowed broad practice discretion within these parameters. For the policy maker, the issue—by contrast—is expressed in terms of situation-specific constituent satisfaction, collegial support, or cooption; in short, a time-limited mandate subject to shifting coalitional support, trade-offs, and political "serendipity" (Kirkpatrick et al., 1976). Regardless of its basis, goal agreement is an underlying dimension in the perception of political feasibility (Van Horn, and Van Meter, 1975: 460; Bolan, 1969: 306).

For the moment, we will again ignore this perceptual dichotomy and stimulus for action and call the variable "*Political Complexity.*"

Solution Agreement

Finally, decision makers must consider solution strategies. For our purposes, a key aspect of solutions is technical feasibility described in the literature as knowledge of causation (Thompson, 1967: 83), analyzability (Kotter and Lawrence, 1974: 130), or calculability.

For the policy maker, the essence of solutions is "Does it work?"—both in terms of socially accepted improvement and in a summative cost/benefit sense. For the program administrator, the issue is largely a matter of relative improvement determined by available organizational resources and the state of technical knowledge—in other words, professional wisdom. Once again ignoring these distinctions, we can call this summary variable "*Technical Complexity.*"

Taken together, these decision dimensions can be calibrated from low to high and produce the decision-making paradigm shown in Figure 1.

For purposes of illustration, we can exemplify programs compatible with these dimensions as follows:

(1) low Scale, low Political Complexity, low Technical Complexity, leading to voluntary program implementation (for example, voter registration, Goodwill Industries, etc.);

(2) low Scale, low Political Complexity, high Technical Complexity, leading to voluntary experimental and pilot programs (such as auditory training programs within a school for the hearing impaired, "Meals on wheels" nutrition programs for a community's senior citizens, etc.);

(3) low Scale, high Political Complexity, low Technical Complexity, leading to avoidance until some crisis provokes a response which may then be token (as in personal use of state telephone lines for legislators, assignment of *Myra Breckenridge* to a high school literature class, etc., followed by token restrictions—of course, it is possible that more severe reactions could follow, in which case examples should be modified);

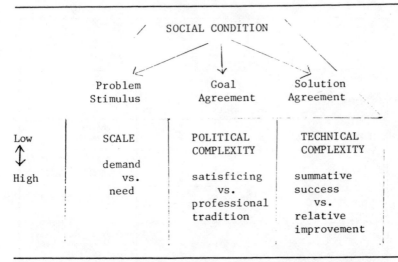

Figure 1: Decisionmaking Variables for Policymakers and Program Administrators

(4) low Scale, high Political Complexity, high Technical Complexity, leading to avoidance until some crisis provokes a response which likely will become a protracted controversy, (for example, city zoning changes in order to accommodate community-based programs for the developmentally disabled, or location of community correctional facilities);

(5) high Scale, low Political Complexity, low Technical Complexity, leading to large-scale implementation programs (the national school lunch program and voter registration);

(6) high Scale, high Political Complexity, high Technical Complexity, leading to negotiated, controversial programs, (such as the swine flu prevention program);

(7) high Scale, low Political Complexity, high Technical Complexity, leading to large-scale national experimental and design programs (of which the national space race is a prime example); and finally,

(8) high scale, high Political Complexity, low Technical Complexity, leading to log-rolling and incremental programming (for example, the tax-supported abortion issue as it is being implemented—and not implemented—within individual states.

These examples are not intended to be exhaustive nor are the variables presumed to be the only factors influencing decision-

	SCALE		POLITICAL COMPLEXITY		TECHNICAL COMPLEXITY		PROGRAM RESPONSE
	low	high	low	high	low	high	
1.	X		X		X		voluntary program implementation
2.	X		X			X	voluntary experimental and pilot programs
3.	X			X	X		avoidance until crisis (token)
4.	X			X		X	avoidance until crisis (protracted controversy)
5.		X	X		X		large scale implementation
6.		X	X			X	negotiated controversial programs
7.		X	X			X	large scale national experimental & design programs
8.		X	X		X		logrolling and incremental programming

Figure 2: Some Examples of Program Responses to Decision Variables

making. Rather, they illustrate our simplified proposed decision-making paradigm through which differential actor responses may be examined. So far we have addressed decision making largely in terms of policy makers and program administrators/implementors. Now it is useful to introduce planners and evaluators.

RELATIONSHIP BETWEEN DECISION VARIABLES AND PLANNING AND EVALUATION STRATEGIES

A variety of literatures are provocative in postulating certain ideal congruencies between planning strategies and evaluation criteria. These, in turn, provide a framework for the examination of typical actor responses.

Prop. 2: *The smaller the perceived scale of the problem, the greater the likelihood of voluntary action with little or no authoritative planning and a reliance upon activity reports as the evaluation criterion.*

Prop. 3: *The lower the technical complexity, the greater the likelihood of comprehensive rational planning and outcome-oriented summative evaluation (Scriven, 1967) based on absolute, empirical criteria due to known causal relationships and relatively predictable future events toward which planning can be directed.*

Prop. 4: *The greater the technical complexity, the greater the likelihood of incremental planning and formative evaluation (Scriven, 1967) for organizational experiments and learning.*

Prop. 5: *The greater the political complexity, the greater the disjointed incremental planning and the greater the dispute over evaluation methodologies which at best will be based on negotiated standards and criteria (Green, 1977).*

These agreements for "fit" between planning and evaluation strategies are consistent with a number of paradigms. Thompson (1967: 92) suggests that organizations respond to demands for rational assessment with certain preferences for the criteria against which they will be judged. To the extent that outcomes are agreed upon ("crystallized"), empirical criteria will be selected to demonstrate either efficiency/effectiveness or that an instrumental state of affairs has been achieved. By contrast, where desired outcomes are ambiguous, social referents and comparative assessments are likely to be preferred.

Likewise, these arguments are consistent with the decisional research explored by Pfeffer et al. (1976). In disciplines and fields characterized by a history of scientific evidence establishing causes of success and failure, empirical referents were used largely to make decisions about resource allocations. In contrast, "unparadigmatically developed" fields relied more on social referents either as sources of information regarding the "best" alternative or because a particular choice would result in a valuable increase in prestige or power.

THE DILEMMA OF PLANNING UTILITIES—
PROFESSIONAL ROLES AND PERSONAL RULES

Unfortunately, the above argument for "fit" is more ideal than descriptive of the interaction between these role sets. This brings us to the next critical question: How do policy makers, planners, program implementors, and evaluators see themselves? Although self-profiles are rare in the literature, there are a few clues.

With respect to policy makers, Kotter and Lawrence (1974) describe five types of mayors; each one uses his personal and interpersonal skills to varying degrees with varying success depending upon his stylistic fit with the city's character. But the essential currency is *influence*. Likewise, Lerner (1976: 20) defines the "politico" as the person "with an institutional position of authority in a system that leads him to consciously manipulate human relationships in order to achieve goals." The point is that policy makers rely on strategies of interpersonal interactions to both define demand and maintain power. Their utility or primary value is *Political Advantage*.

With respect to planners, Dyckman (1973: 244) mentions the increasing role of social science in planning curricula, with its rationalistic bias. Myerson observes:

> The planner is a full time professional in a field marked by technical standards of achievement for the evaluation of performances; operates in the absence of conventional profit motives, with the presumption that he will be sparing in the intrusion of his own value and will venerate "objectivity" [Myerson, 19   ].

The key phrase is *Objective Need Assessment*.

Program implementors, directors, or administrators suggest a variety of stereotypes. Patton (1978) suggests that they operate in stark contrast to social scientists, who prefer testing abstract models of sociocultural behavior; instead, they desire tests of their own, often implicit theories. Their professional activity is primarily devoted to linking people ("clients") to resources through a comparatively high reliance on precedent, common sense, and intuition (Glaser et al., 1976). The key phrase is *Organizational Advantage*.

Finally we come to evaluators. Like the other actors in this model, they emanate from diverse fields, but share some training in scientific research methodology and program experience (Weiss, 1977: 184; Patton, 1978: 15) The key phrase here is *Objective Evaluation*.

To sum, policy makers and program directors are more likely to make decisions from *social references*. Planners and evaluators are more likely to employ empirical criteria. In the absence of clear-cut diagnostics each role set will opt for decision criteria consistent with its own ideology, but in conflict with professional integration.

Of course, these portraits are stereotypic. Nonetheless, social problems are defined—at least in part—by desired end states. End states, solutions, or policies may be generated, however, from at least two sources: (1) by the application of one's skills and professional training and/or (2) by the infusion of one's values. Rein (1971: 298), in fact, suggests that the latter is ever-present:

How do values intrude into the analysis of policy? The first, and most obvious intrusion is the way analysts define the purposes of policy. This asserts for them what is morally right. Second, systems of beliefs are seldom mutually reinforcing or internally consistent. More typically, the various aspects of these values prove in practice to be in partial conflict with each other. Thus, ideology must address the demanding task of sorting priorities for action. Third, people attach as much ideological importance to form as they do to purpose, so in time they ask not whether an institution is relevant to society, but how society can change to enable that institution to perform. Fourth, analysts of policy are specifically concerned with being useful and this preoccupation with political feasibility may affect their interpretation of values. Values can be subordinated to the pragmatic sense of what is possible, accepting a preferred solution within the limits of feasibility, or can lead to commitment to altering the political climate, and thus extending the range of acceptable policies.

Finally, values influence the ways in which outcomes are interpreted not only in the measures used to assess change, but also in the implications to be drawn from the outcomes to which attention is directed.

Hence, skills *and* values function as comingled decisional criteria.

Frequently the alignment between one's professional problem-solving skills, values, and the nature of the social problem is congruent and even across actors there is a kind of compatibility. For example, in the earlier example #5 (see Figure 2), a national school lunch program is likely to be favorable to politician's constituents. It is also a routine technology that lends itself to high analyzability for planning, implementation, and evaluation.

However, incompatibility in terms of a shared problem-solving approach seems more probable. This is illustrated by event #6 (see Figure 2), the swine flu example. One should recall that solution strategies were dramatically disparate. First, the degree of need—*Scale*—was disputed between the scientific estimates from the medical community and the political planning staffs within the Executive Office. *Technical Feasibility* was also contested; pharmaceutical companies insisted that demands could be met which matched acceptable margins of safety with the magnitude of production. Independent scientists expressed other opinions. Implementors—in this case primarily the state public health directors—caught between governmental mandates and scientific dispute, vacillated in their compliance. It is a lucid example of the variance between the empiric, "econological" (Thompson and Tuden, 1959: 195) standards and the political-social logic.

To sum, we have proposed that individual actors are likely to operate within two sets of decision rules, their professional training logic and their personal values. In addition, any individual may adhere to the mandates of one source of decision logic or the other, most probably a less-than-conscious combination of both. Achieving integrated decision making—that is, expanding the bounds of current decisional rationality—demands analytic and behavioral skills beyond knowledge of variables and utilities. Yet another factor, the decision type, previously advanced by Thompson and Tuden (1959), is critical.

DECISION TYPES AND
STRATEGIES FOR PROGRAM DEVELOPMENT

Thompson and Tuden (1959) postulated that decision makers needed not only to understand the type of decision arena in which they are engaged, but also would benefit from matching decision-making strategies and organizational decision sets to the problem type. This model is summarized in Figure 3a.

Given the reality of multiple daily pressures, one would expect that in most situations decision makers would prefer the "computational" decision, presumably the easiest of all decision types. But even that hypothetical quadrant is not reached without some effort. The reader should recall that we have thus far considered another dimension: a "precondition," to decision making: *Scale*. Combining that with our other variables we can modify the Thompson-Tuden model and summarize problem perception preferences on the part of each set of actors (see Figure 4.) This illustrates that the presence of perceptual differences operates on —and obstructs—conjoint problem perception, definition of decision type, and resulting solution designs.

While the "computational" quadrant should (conceptually, at least) maximize the preferences and ideologies of all actors, the remaining possible decision contexts meet the preferences of only subsets of actors.

Under conditions of *Political Complexity*, the Thompson and Tuden model would argue for *compromise* (see Figure 3a). While the policy maker might feel adept in such a circumstance, it is an unhappy situation for program administrators who would like the comfort and economics of prior success associated with "one best way." This gives rise to several speculative propositions concerning program development:

Prop. 6: Under the condition of political complexity:

(a) Program administrators who "sell" a single program modality will experience:

- *tenuous or ephemeral resource support in the absence of a powerful and long-standing advocate group, and*
- *scapegoating by policy makers of the single programmatic solution obtained from dissatisfied clients as a means of building their own constituent—and adversarial—support.*

(b) Policy makers who "buy" a single program modality will experience:

- *evaluation indicating less client participation and/or satisfaction than is politically desirable and*

Preference About Possible
Outcomes

		Agreement	Non-Agreement
Beliefs About Causation	Agreement	Computation in Bureaucratic Structure	Bargaining in Representative Structure
	Non-Agreement	Majority Judgment in Collegial Structure	Inspiration or Charasmatic Leadership in Anomic Structure

Figure 3a: The Thompson and Tuden (1959) Typology of Decision Types and Processes

<u>What</u> is the expert solution? <u>Who</u> are the expert(s) to design the solution strategy?	Toward what end(s)-<u>why</u>-should we do what we are doing?
<u>How</u> should we best obtain our shared goal(s)?	<u>Why</u>, <u>what</u> and <u>how</u> can we get out of this dilemma?

Figure 3b: Typical Diagnostic Questions Relevant to Decision Types

- scapegoating of policy as being "unresponsive" to the continuum of citizen concerns.

(c) Planners in this circumstance will profit—in terms of utilization of plans—from a focus on highlighting client differences and "equitable" (proportional) alternatives.

(d) Evaluators will benefit from consideration of client preferences and satisfaction as well as technological assessment.

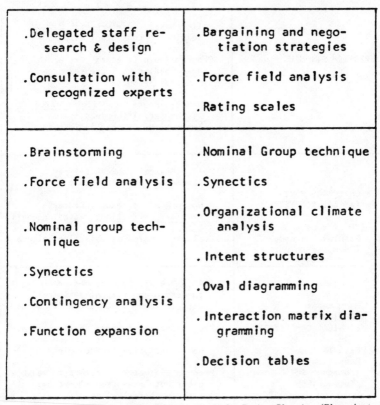

.Delegated staff research & design .Consultation with recognized experts	.Bargaining and negotiation strategies .Force field analysis .Rating scales
.Brainstorming .Force field analysis .Nominal group technique .Synectics .Contingency analysis .Function expansion	.Nominal Group technique .Synectics .Organizational climate analysis .Intent structures .Oval diagramming .Interaction matrix diagramming .Decision tables

Note: Adapted from Delp et al., *Systems Tools for Project Planning*, (Bloomington: International Development Institute, 1977).

Figure 3c: Possible Decision Strategies Relevant to Decision Types

In a world where decision makers prefer the simplification of tradition rather than diversity (Mintzberg, 1976), our admonitions provide little comfort. Yet overreliance on single program modalities or exaggerated claims at meeting "all needs" leads to doubt and cynicism about professional wisdom. It also stimulates countervailing power (Galbraith, 1967)—versus shared problem-lving—as the mechanism by which freedom of choice among alternatives is created or restored. It is perhaps in this very case that program administrators, planners, and evaluators must be most responsive and reactive—rather than proactive—to the

PROBLEM STIMULUS "SCALE"	Policy Maker: prefers high <u>Demand</u> leading to consistent support Program Administrator: Prefers high <u>Need</u> leading to increased organi- aztional resources Planner: Prefers <u>Undifferentiated Client Definition</u> leading to quantified SES need indicators
GOAL AGREEMENT "POLITICAL COMPLEXITY" ("Preferences About Possible Outcomes" (Thompson & Tuden, 1959)	Policy Maker: Prefers <u>Citizen Agreement</u> regarding goals Program Administrator: Prefers <u>Provider Definitions</u> regarding goals Evaluator: Aims at objective balance
means SOLUTION AGREEMENT "TECHNICAL COMPLEXITY" "Beliefs About Causation", (Thompson & Tuden, 1959)	Policy Maker: Prefers "assurance" of success & constituent satisfaction with outcomes in Cost/Benefit terms Program Administrator: Prefers stand- ardized, large-scale, proven and non-descriptive technologies Program Evaluator: Prefers to measure clear cut 'measureable' outcomes with quantitative techniques

Figure 4: Summary of Actor Perception Preferences which Influence Problem Per- ception, Definition of Decision Type, and Resulting Solution Strategies

political realities of fragile compromises sensitively negotiated by policy makers. These "compromises" may appear to be controversial in light of normative professional practices focused on technical/professional criteria. But they may represent exactly the "bounded rationality" (Simon, 1957) necessary and appro- priate under this condition. Program development, under con- ditions of *Political Complexity*, will fare better through negoti- ated solution strategies which incorporate political concerns than through reliance on professional precedent subjected to continual political harassment.

Prop. 7: *Under conditions of technical complexity, rationality is facilitated by judgmental decision making (Thompson and Tuden, 1959). This means that program administrators must modify their favored program mode to encompass developmental planning, pilot studies, and comparative evaluation of demonstrations.*

The practice of such technology, well known to program administrators, is not without high risk, high cost, and long time spans for learning. But these very conditions subject administrators/implementors to numerous pressures for premature conclusions from policy makers who are anxious to truncate the time before payoffs, power, and profit can be proclaimed. It is not surprising, then, that both policy makers and program administrators often lack "patience" with such efforts. Planners need to be careful not to be coopted into arguing for enlarged resources based on need *prior* to solution development. Evaluators need to beware of serving as premature "hatchet men," defining summative cost-benefits without consideration of the benefit of formative logic associated with early experimental projects for solution development. Such innovation remains a fragile exercise which inappropriate evaluation can perniciously destroy.

Some speculative propositions apropos to *Technical Complicity* include:

(a) Decisionmaking in this mode should be judgmental—that is, the outcome of "experts" who, lacking an absolute solution due to the absence of clear-cut cause and effect, can knowledgeably pool their wisdom. Policy makers would do well to distance themselves from specific decisions, delegating to research groups and venture groups the mandate for specific experiments to determine at least the relative effectiveness of alternative "means"—methods of treatment or service delivery—if not cause and effect. Political fortunes will thus not rise and fall on short-run results.

(b) Program administrators should base advocacy on technical complexity and general indication of need. Detailed need assessment is premature. Indeed, qualitative understanding of complexities is perhaps more seminal. "Overselling" results on client service to obtain large resources will lead to a sense of betrayal on the part of the policy makers.

(c) Evaluators should stress formative evaluation (Scriven, 1967) to enhance organizational learning as well as comparative evaluation between treatment or service methodologies to determine relative benefits. Effectiveness must precede efficiency, but the tradeoff is small-scale experimentation.

This leaves Thompson and Tuden's "Charismatic" quadrant where both *Political Complexity* and *Technical Complexity* interact. An interesting variant of this circumstance is where a modest problem stimulus (Small *Scale*) is insufficient for *demand* consensus from policy makers, but large enough to stimulate *need* perception among a subset of program administrators. This is precisely the situation of many small delivery organizations serving a politically weak client group. Such programs must act on the following strategies to legitimize their existence:

(1) Rely on patronage from policy makers who have some "personal experience with the problem.

(2) Utilize "charisma" to raise social consciousness so that the client group's need becomes an ethical demand (Rothman, 1974: 338).

(3) Utilize community organization as a planning variant to increase *demand* (Rothman, 1974: 326-398).

(4) Become an experimental program using experimental modes to develop technologies which can be transferred to large need groups.

Figure 5 summarizes in a normative paradigm consultant recommendations for policy, planning, program management, and evaluation. The diagnostic dimensions of *Scale, Political Complexity,* and *Technical Complexity* are coupled with modes of policy and strategies for implementation, planning, and evaluation.

SUMMARY

Under conditions of complexity, either political or technical, the tendency for each role set is to opt for its own favorite profes-

DECISIONMAKING CONTEXT

SCALE		TECHNICAL COMPLEXITY		POLITICAL COMPLEXITY		RECOMMENDATIONS TO INCREASE RATIONALITY
low	high	low	high	low	high	
X		X		X		adopt "utilization focused evaluation approach" (Patton, 1978)
X		X			X	avoid single program modality legitimate need adopt utilization focused evaluation which includes summative modes
X			X	X		legitimate need through experimental strategies which are relevant for larger groups
X			X		X	develop alternate plans recognizing differences, negotiate solution strategies, focus on formative, comparative evaluations which attend to client differences and satisfactions
	X	X		X		optimal condition for rational planning & summative evaluation
	X	X			X	modify single program solution strategies to political reality
	X		X	X		implement experimental solution strategies to determine cause-effect relationships
	X		X		X	negotiate through judgmental decisionmaking for organizational learning

ACTOR PREFERENCES FOR PROPOSED OUTCOMES

Programs: Voluntary action
Planning: little/none
Evaluation: Process/Activity reports
: large scale program response contingent on mediated political/technical decision-making

Programs: contingent on political stake holders
Planning: comprehensive rational
Evaluation: summative evaluation
: experimental pilot programs
: incremental planning
: formative evaluation

Programs: either large scale programs or no programs dependent on demand
Planning: rational planning dependent on technical complexity
Evaluation: evaluation mode dependent on technical complexity
: conflict between empirical and social logics
: disjointed, incremental planning
: negotiated evaluation if any

Figure 5: Summary Recommendations for Integrated Program Development Efforts

sional and/or traditional logic at the expense of the logic of others. While the imposition of this professionally induced normative position is an effective way of reducing ambiguity and simplifying complex situations, that resolution is simply ephemeral: It leaves any particular position vulnerable to attack from the perspective of other traditions. What is, therefore, *particularly* important—although intuitively and even professionally undesirable—is for someone to mediate the various perspectives to induce shared risk and involvement. Mediated, purposeful exploration of alternate perspectives can become a mechanism for mollifying reactionary scapegoating, exploitation, and defensiveness engendered by unidimensional ideologies. It is simply unlikely that even well-conceived comprehensive programs will work out terribly well under complexity. Expectations under these conditions will have to be much more tentative, much more experimental, promise less, and lead to organizational learning as opposed to some magic solution. Unless as a society we are willing to endure periods of learning and share the risks and expense of that learning—as opposed to attacking the limited results during learning periods from the ideological base of one's own preferred norms—we invariably destroy the resiliency and willingness of the various organizational actors to respond to complex circumstances. It leads to simplification, rhetoric, and attack, none of which creates an environment in which complex problems can be fruitfully addressed.

It has been the purpose of this chapter to suggest that each of us, as professionals in program development, needs to be aware of these dialectics. Without mediation they will proceed much like a Greek tragedy where good people following the best logic of their own particular perceptions are vulnerable, where inexorably they will be discredited by someone operating out of a separate tradition, and where problems prevail over learning and success. Resolutions of contemporary complexities call for both sensitivity to the alternate paradigms from which professionals emanate *and* deliberate contingent problem-solving strategies to mediate the political/program/planning risks associated with the more experimental attitude.

SUMMARY OF PROPOSITIONS

Prop. 1: Throughout the drama of program development, each actor—policy maker, planner, program implementor, and evaluator—tends to respond to decision elements (problem stimulus, goal agreement, and solution agreement) from a different perceptual "set" or basis, which leads to inter-actor variance in terms of preferred solution strategies or outcomes.

Prop. 2: The smaller the perceived scale of the problem, the greater the likelihood of voluntary action with little or no authoritative planning and a reliance upon activity reports as the evaluation criterion.

Prop. 3: The lower the technical complexity, the greater the likelihood of comprehensive rational planning and outcome-oriented summative evaluation based on absolute, empirical criteria due to known causal relationships and relatively predictable future events toward which planning can be directed.

Prop. 4: The greater the technical complexity, the greater the likelihood of incremental planning and formative evaluation for organizational experiments and learning.

Prop. 5: The greater the political complexity, the greater the disjointed incremental planning and the greater the dispute over evaluation methodologies which at best will be based on negotiated standards and criteria.

Prop. 6: Under the condition of political complexity:

    (a) Program administrators who "sell" a single program modality will experience:

- tenuous or ephemeral resource support in the absence of a powerful and long-standing advocate group, and
- scapegoating by policy makers of the single programmatic solution obtained from dissatisfied clients as a means of building their own consituent—and adversarial—support.

    (b) Policy makers who "buy" a single program modality will experience:

- evaluations indicating less client participation or satisfaction than is politically desirable and
- scapegoating of policy as being "unresponsive" to the continuum of citizen concerns.

    (c) Planners in this circumstance will profit—in terms of utilization of plans—from a focus on highlighting client differences and "equitable", (proportional) alternatives.

    (d) Evaluators will benefit from consideration of client preferences and satisfaction as well as technological assessment.

Prop. 7: Under conditions of technical complexity, rationality is facilitated by judgmental decision making. This means that program administrators must modify their favored program mode to encompass developmental planning, pilot studies, and comparative evaluations of demonstrations.

    (a) Decision making in this mode should be judgmental —that is, the outcome of "experts" who, lacking an absolute solution due to the absence of clear-cut cause and effect, can knowledgeably pool their wisdom. Policy makers would do well to distance themselves from specific decisions, delegating to research groups and venture groups the mandate for specific experiments to determine at least the relative effectiveness of alternate "means"—methods of treatment or service delivery—if not cause and effect. Political fortunes will thus not rise on short-run results.

    (b) Program administrators should base advocacy on technical complexity and general indication of need. Detailed need assessment is premature. Indeed, qualitative understanding of complexities is perhaps more seminal. "Overselling" results in client service

    more seminal. "Overselling" results on client service to obtain large resources will lead to a sense of betrayal on the part of the policy makers.

    (c) Evaluators should stress formative evaluation to enhance organizational learning as well as comparative evaluation between treatment or service methodologies to determine relative benefits. Effectiveness must precede efficiency, but the trade-off is small-scale experimentation.

Prop. 8: Where the political complexity interacts with technical complexity along with small scale, programs must legitimate their existence:

    (a) Rely on patronage from policy makers who have some "personal" experience with the problem.

    (b) Utilize "charisma" to raise social consciousness so that the client group's need becomes an ethical demand.

(c) Utilize community organization as a planning variant to increase demand.

(d) Become an experimental program using experimental modes to develop technologies which can be transferred to larger need groups.

REFERENCES

ANDERSON, J. E. (1975) Public Policy-Making. New York: Praeger.

BOLAN, R. S. (1971) "Generalist within a specialty—still valid? Educating the urban planner: An expert on experts." In Ch. 3, Planning 1971: Selected Papers From the ASPO Planning Conference. American Society of Planning Officials.

——— (1969) "Community decision behavior: The culture of planning." American Institute of Planners Journal (September):301-330.

CAPLAN N. (1977) "A minimal set of conditions necessary for the utilization of social science knowledge in policy formulation at the national level." In C. H. Weiss, Using Social Research in Public Policy-Making. Lexington, MA: D.C. Heath.

CUNNINGHAM, J. B. (1977) "Approaches to the evaluation of organizational effectiveness." Academy of Management Review 2(July):463-474.

DELP, P., A. THESEN, J. MOTIWALLA, and N. SESHADRI (1977) Systems Tools for Project Planning. Bloomington: International Development Institute, Indiana University.

DYCKMAN, J. W. (1973) "What makes planners plan?" In A. Faludi (ed.), A Reader in Planning Theory. New York: Pergamon.

FRIEDMANN, J. (1969) "Notes on societal action." American Institute of Planners Journal (September): 311-318.

GALBRAITH, J. K. (1967) The New Industrial State. Boston: Houghton Mifflin.

GLASER, E. et al. (1976) "Putting knowledge to use: a distillation of the literature regarding knowledge transfer and change." Los Angeles: Human Interaction Research Institute.

GREEN, L. (1977) "Big effects in health research: how would we ever know if we got one?" Presented at the first annual meeting of the Evaluation Research Society, October 13-15.

KIRKPATRICK, S. A., D. F. DAVIS, and R. D. ROBERTSON (1976) "The process of political decision-making in groups: search behavior and choice shifts." American Behavioral Scientist 20 (September/October).

KOTTER, J. P. and P. R. LAWRENCE (1974) Mayors in Action: Five Approaches to Urban Governance. New York: John Wiley.

LERNER, A. W. (1976) The Politics of Decision-Making: Strategy, Cooperation and Conflict. Beverly Hills, CA: Sage.

MAJONE, G. (1977) "On the notion of political feasibility." in S. S. Nagel (ed.), Policy Studies Review Annual (Vol. 1). Beverly Hills, CA: Sage.

MINTZBERG, H., D. RAISINGHANI, and A. THEORET (1976) "The structure of 'unstructured' decision processes."." Administration Science Quarterly (June): 246-275.

PATTON, M. Q. (1978) A Utilization Focused Approach to Evaluation. Beverly Hills, CA: Sage.

PARENTI, M. (1974) "Power and pluralism: a view from the bottom." In D. F. Mazotti, "The underlying assumptions of advocacy planning: pluralism and reform." American Institute of Planners Journal (January):43.

PERKINS, D.N.T. (1977) "Evaluating social interventions: a conceptual schema." Evaluation Quarterly 1(November):139-656.

PFEFFER, J. G., R. SALANCIK, and HUSEY (1976) In Leblabici, "The effects of uncertainty on the use of social influence in organizational decision making." Administrative Science Quarterly (June):231.

RAKOFF, S. H. and G. F. SCHAEFER (1970) "Politics, policy, and political science: theoretical alternatives." Policy and Society (November):51-78.

REIN, M. (1971) "Social policy analysis as the interpretation of beliefs." American Institute of Planners Journal (September):297-310.

ROTHMAN, J. (1974) Planning and Organizing for Social Change: Action Principles from Social Science Research. New York: Columbia University Press.

SCRIVEN, M. S. (1967) The Methodology of Evaluation, (AERA monograph series on Curriculum Evaluation, Book I). Chicago: Rand McNally.

SIMON, H. (1973) In T.J. Cartwright, "Problems, solutions and strategies: a contribution to the theory and practice of planning." American Institute of Planners Journal (May): 179-187.

——— (1957) Administrative Behavior: A Study of Decision-Making in Administrative Organization." New York: Free Press.

THOMPSON, J. D. (1967) Organizations in Action. New York: McGraw-Hill.

——— and A. TUDEN (1959) "Strategies, structures and processes of organizational

decision." In Comparative Studies in Administration. Pittsburgh: University of Pittsburgh Press.

VAN HORN, C. E. and D. S. VAN METER (1975) "The policy implementation process: a conceptual framework." Administration & Society 6 (February):445-488.

WEISS, C. H. [ed.] (1977) Using Social Research in Public Policy Making. Lexington, MA: D.C. Heath.

Charles Windle
National Institute of Mental Health

Ann Majchrzak
University of California, Los Angeles

Eugenie Walsh Flaherty
Philadelphia Health Management Corp.

2

PROGRAM EVALUATION AT THE
INTERFACE OF PROGRAM ECHELONS

Advocates of program evaluation often argue for its desirability in abstract, idealized terms, without distinguishing among types of program or management echelons. It is likely that such distinctions are important and, further, that the relationship between management echelons influences types of program evaluation undertaken and the utilization of evaluation results.

The program evaluation activities of the National Institute of Mental Health (NIMH) over the past nine years provide an opportunity to see how program evaluation activities vary with the relationship between program echelons. These observations can be based on two types of experience: (a) NIMH's use of funds

AUTHORS' NOTE: *This chapter is based on a paper presented at the Evaluation Research Society Meeting, Washington, D.C., November 2, 1978. The views expressed are those of the authors and not necessarily those of the National Institute of Mental Health.*

specifically set aside for the evaluation of NIMH's own programs and (b) study of the program evaluation in federally funded Community Mental Health Centers (CMHC) before and after Congress required centers to do program evaluation.

NIMH's EVALUATION EFFORT

The Experience of Using Evaluation Results

NIMH's effort to evaluate its own programs has been fairly extensive. Beginning in 1969 special funds were made available for program evaluation as part of the CMHC Act. This authority was expanded by a 1970 Amendment to Section 513 of the Public Health Service Act authorizing expenditure of up to one percent of any appropriation for program evaluation. The major program NIMH evaluated was the CMHC Program, on which approximately 50 studies have been performed by contracts costing about $4 million. Many of these studies were idealistically conceived to improve the program by examining ways NIMH could help centers attain the program's service process goals (Windle et al., 1974). Other studies were concerned with program viability—answering questions about how well the program functions of aiding Congress to see that the virtues of the program merited more money. Some funds were also used to support longer-run evaluations by developing methods which could be used for future NIMH studies. Finally, some contracts were aimed at improving centers' management by aiding local centers in evaluating their own services.

Although the range of studies funded was broad, NIMH's use of this investment has been rather narrow. It has been limited to two main areas, one directed at a lower echelon (local centers) and the other directed at a higher echelon (the U.S. Congress). First, since 1970 NIMH has given substantial aid to centers on how to perform program evaluation (Bass and Windle, 1972; Hagedorn et al., 1976; Hargreaves et al., 1977; Montague and Taylor, 1971; Reidel et al., 1974; Rosen et al., 1975; Sorensen and Phipps, 1972). This assistance was timely, since Congress later required centers to perform program evaluation. Second, NIMH passed on to Congress the results of studies which indicated that centers needed continued funding beyond the original limits on seed money grants in order to be viable.

Apart from these broad uses, the bulk of the information from the substantive evaluations was not used by NIMH to improve the program (Stockdill and Sharfstein, 1976; Windle and Bates, 1974). Nor was there a concerted effort to put substantive evaluation results into an educational format and distribute them to regional offices, states, or individual centers for their use. Moreover, although NIMH prepared to respond to requests for information, little was done to tell centers what information was available and how it might be useful.

NIMH's neglect of evaluation results did not mean there was no ultimate use. Other investigators, such as Nader's Center for the Study of Responsive Law (Chu and Trotter, 1974) and the U.S. General Accounting Office (1974), used these studies as data in their own evaluations of NIMH's program, bringing them into the general policy analysis literature. This form of indirect dissemination has the advantage of adding credibility to the results. However, to be timely and complete, it should supplement direct dissemination rather than replace it.

Observations and Suggestions

Given the fact that NIMH mandated program evaluation relevant to the programs it funds, one might legitimately ask why the use of this evaluation information for program improvement was relatively low. The reasons seem to fall into two categories: (a) a perceived need by bureaucrats to protect the program they are a part of and (b) a natural antagonism to authority.

PROTECTING THE PROGRAM

In general, it is fair to say that program administrators feel a need to defend their programs; this is especially true when the program in question has the potential for growth. For NIMH this seemed to be particularly true since the Nixon-Ford administration threatened to end the CMHC program—a threat which required mobilization for defense rather than reform (Stockdill and Sharfstein, 1976).

The phenomenon of "protection" is also traceable to "natural antagonisms" or goal conflicts between program echelons (Katz, 1977). These conflicts may take the form of a difference in values which are adhered to at one level of the bureaucracy and not another (Weiss, 1975). In other words, what is success at one echelon may be failure at another.

Alternatively, the tension may relate to the many and varied purposes of program evaluation. Neigher (forthcoming) has described three purposes for program evaluation: amelioration, advocacy, and accountability. Amelioration usually assumes that decisions will be made at the level of the program being evaluated. The other two are complementary views of decisions expected to be made at a higher level, decisions usually related to program support. Advocacy occurs when a program's support is deemed most important (reflecting mainly the program's interests); accountability, when the program's obligations are the priority (reflecting the funders' concerns).

Beyond the factors just discussed, it is critical to underscore a conclusion which is prominent in the literature on bureaucracy: Organizations are resistant to change. In addition, it has been observed that organizations which are loosely or collectively organized and which depend heavily on outsiders have difficulty making changes directed toward overall improvement (Roos, 1974), and are most likely to use evaluation for advocacy and accountability purposes. NIMH acted in this fashion, and the conditions in many public service organizations make this orientation frequent. Inability to make self-improvements may be what has been called lack of evaluability (Wholey et al., 1975) or organizational readiness for evaluation (Kiresuk et al., 1977).

Katz (1977) has described how the natural antagonisms of authority internal and external to organizations result in organizations trying to strengthen their internal control by protecting members from external authority. These protections become corrupt when, "instead of strengthening the authority of persons in officially superordinate positions" to pursue the organization's goals, they "strengthen the independent authority and illegitimate purposes of the persons granted lenience." Thus, the conditions of the organization vis-a-vis outsiders can seriously blunt the interest of the organization in using program evaluation information for program improvement.

STRATEGIES FOR FACILITATING UTILIZATION

NIMH's experience suggests that more mechanisms need to be built into program evaluation systems to strengthen programs' use of evaluation information. These mechanisms should deal with dissemination of the results of studies, preparation and distribution of agency plans to use (or not use) study results, and should require follow-up reports on this use. The mechanisms have to be set and enforced by a higher-echelon office. For NIMH, this should be the Secretary of the Department of Health, Education and Welfare (HEW) or the Office of Management and Budget. This central focal point would also lead to a wider distribution of evaluation results (Bernstein and Freeman, 1975).

HEW has taken steps to make reports available to the public on request, but most supervisory attention in the past has gone into controlling the initiation of evaluation studies. Such control seems desirable to assure that important issues are dealth with, designs are relatively unbiased and feasible, and that related studies are coordinated. However, in practice this control seems to undermine thoughtful development of contracts by delaying approvals of concepts until late in each fiscal year.

For agency evaluation to lead to program improvement, higher echelons should give more attention to the *use* of evaluation results. The approval process should require convincing plans and evidence of program management commitment for using study results. This requirement would increase the public benefit from evaluation studies, and would restrict the flow of money into evaluations under a sensible rather than a frustrating rationale.

Local Centers' Evaluations: The Experience

While NIMH's use of its own program evaluation results has been limited, NIMH has advocated enthusiastically its use within CMHCs and has done much to increase centers' abilities to evaluate. When the CMHC Program began, *Research and Evalu-*

ation was specified as an optional service eligible for federal support. As program critics pointed out ways to improve the CMHC Program, program evaluation was identified as one way for centers to improve their own management (Chu and Trotter, 1974; U.S. General Accounting Office, 1974). In the CMHC Amendments of 1975, Congress required all centers to do program self-evaluation, and made this requirement specific by listing topics to be included in the evaluation (Windle and Ochberg, 1975).

Majchrzak and Windle (n.d.) examined the types of program evaluations performed by 181 centers in 1973, before program evaluation was required. These results were derived from a mail questionnaire completed by the centers included in this study. The types of evaluation activities reported include: evaluation of client satisfaction, evaluation of community problems, evaluation of client change, evaluation of costs, information on client statistics, information on continuity of care, information on utilization of services, and information on client complaints (see Table 1).[1] In total, the centers included in this study reported 24 different types of evaluation activities. These types were factor analyzed to determine if there were any "patterns" in the various evaluation approaches used by CMHCs. There appeared to be several types of both process and outcome evaluations that were identified through our analysis. In addition, client complaint and utilization review were also identified as types of evaluation. In sum, eight orthogonal factors were identified (see Table 1).

One might not expect CMHCs to perform complex evaluations at an early stage of development. Hargreaves (1975) found, however, that 51 community care organizations in California, Nevada, Arizona, and Hawaii typically had not developed sufficiently by 1973 to do difficult evaluations.

The factor analysis was supplemented with a "cluster analysis" *pattern* of increasing comprehensiveness of total evaluation efforts (see Table 2).

To compare clusters on the usefulness of their evaluations, we employed answers to the question: "Have any program changes resulted from your program evaluation effort to date?" Three of the clusters could be characterized as having little evaluation

Table 1: Program Evaluation Activities

	Percentage of Variance	Weight on Factor
Factor I. Client Satisfaction	9.1	
Assessing clients' satisfaction with services		.78
Survey of community knowledge, attitudes, and satisfaction		.69
Assessing status of clients several months after termination		.63
Examining premature or staff-disapproved termination rate		.56
Factor II. Community Problems	9.0	
Formal direct surveys of catchment area population for mental health problems		.72
Formal survey of other social agencies for number of persons needing care		.70
Monitoring of social pathology indices (suicides, crime, etc.)		.60
Factor III. Client Change	8.8	
Assessing change in clients during treatment		.84
Assessing change in clients from beginning to end of treatment		.78
Measuring outcome relative to goals by Goal Attainment Scaling		.53
Factor IV. Cost	8.1	
Determining cost of care for an entire facility		.85
Determining cost of care for various types of care		.76
Structured time and motion studies of use of staff time for services		.60
Factor V. Client Statistics	7.3	
Maintaining statistics on location of residence of clients		.76
Maintaining descriptive statistics about clients served		.71
Factor VI. Continuity of Care	7.3	
Monitoring continuity of care within center		.75
Monitoring continuity of care between center and other agencies		.74
Factor VII. Utilization Review	5.4	
Reviewing need for continuing particular services in individual cases		.81
Examining client Utilization Review results for implications for program change		.59
Factor VIII. Client Complaints	5.0	
Publicized client complaint system		.81

NOTE: This table includes all items with loadings over .50 on any factor, except for two items with loadings of .51 and .53 that were not interpretable.

effort, three had moderate evaluation effort, and two had a large or comprehensive evaluation effort. The cluster with greatest emphasis on both Client Change and Client Satisfaction, but least on Client Statistics, reported the lowest impact on program changes. The clusters which emphasized Client Statistics, but neither Client Change nor Client Satisfaction, reported the most impact on program changes. This difference was not present (as the trend was in the opposite direction) among the centers which made more comprehensive program evaluation efforts.[2] This comparison suggests that, at early developmental stages, client statistics, as part of a process type of evaluation, are more likely to be useful in improving programs than outcome types of measures (Client Change or Client Satisfaction).

In studying the impact of evaluation efforts on program changes, the issue of relations between program echelons becomes especially important. The impacts that centers described were classified according to whether the program changes consisted of program reduction, program expansion, or simply changes in ways of operating. Generally, we found that centers reported very few reductions in programs. Almost all reported changes were either program expansions or simply modifications without indication of expansion or contradiction.

The lack of use of evaluation to reduce ineffective activities is somewhat surprising given the growing emphasis on detecting inefficiency and the growing concern with health care costs (Riska and Taylor, 1978). Presumably, many evaluations of center services would be negative if conducted carefully. Mental health service technology is still so primitive that negative or marginal results are not unusual in controlled studies of the efficacy of mental health treatment; centers' goals are likely to be exaggerated to obtain funding; centers' services are often too small to deal with large, multifaceted systematic problems (Weiss, 1970); and staff expectations are shaped by hopes and commitments rather than by sober appraisals (Scheirer, 1978). If evaluation results are indeed negative, it would seem in the public interest to eliminate or reduce some of these programs.

If our data are generalizable beyond our immediate sample, this reduction is not happening or happens only on conjunction with the addition of new program activities. Our finding is con-

Table 2: Proportion of Centers in Each Cluster Performing Each Type of Evaluation Activity

Cluster No.	No. of Strs.	No. of Eval. Activities	Client Satisfaction	Comm. Problems	Cost	Client Statistics	Client Change	Continuity of Care	Summary	% of centers reporting impact
1	25	7	.09	.19	.16	.89	.07	.22	Little evaluation effort, Client Statistics only	52%
14	13	9	.23	.08	.38	.51	.49	.26	Little evaluation effort; attention to Client Change but low on Client Statistics	31%
3	30	9	.09	.18	.72	.82	.09	.40	Little evaluation effort; emphasis on cost and Client Statistics	73%
9	19	11	.50	.21	.31	.81	.28	.60	Moderate evaluation effort; emphasis on Client Satisfaction, Continuity of Care and Client Statistics	73%
8	12	13	.33	.67	.47	.92	.28	.50	Moderate evaluation effort; emphasis on Community Problems, Client Statistics, and Continuity of Care	67%
12	11	14	.38	.21	.88	.91	.41	.86	Moderate evaluation effort; high on most types except Community Problems and Client Satisfaction	73%
2	19	17	.51	.77	.82	.98	.28	.97	Large evaluation effort; high on most types except Client Change	90%
7	12	16	.46	.69	.67	.75	.53	.75	Large evaluation effort touching most types of evaluation	100%

NOTE: Only the six strongest factors are included here.

trary to Schick's suggestion (1971) that program evaluation contrasts with program analysis by being popular in times of lowered program expenditures, rather than in relative prosperity, as a basis for deciding program curtailments rather than expansions. Our results suggest that program evaluation is a means for program expansion much as is program analysis.

Evaluations After 1975

We also looked at centers' program evaluation *after* the CMHC Amendments of 1975 required centers to conduct three types of evaluation activities: quality assurance, self-evaluation on nine topics, and review of their evaluation data with service area residents. The law also requires centers to spend two percent of the prior year's expenditures on evaluation, to submit an annual evaluation report, and to disclose it to the public.

Under contract with NIMH, the Philadelphia Health Management Corporation (1978) examined what evaluation was being done by a stratified sample of nine centers, and how useful or harmful the requirements are to the evaluation efforts of the centers. Most centers had done studies on most of the required topics,[3] sometimes expending great effort. Centers varied widely in the topics they emphasized. Topics also differed in how often they were studied, the effort involved, the reasons they were done, and their judged usefulness. Cost and patterns of service use were viewed as most useful, and were done to meet centers' felt needs for information. Other topics, such as acceptability and inappropriate institutionalization, were done more to comply with external requirements. Centers reported that their evaluation studies of program impact and acceptability of services were more likely to involve "extensive" levels of effort than evaluations of other topics. It is worth noting that there is some agreement between these two studies of centers' evaluation activities in 1973 and 1978 in suggesting that evaluations of client outcome are of low utility relative to their expense.

Centers expressed little interest in citizen involvement in evaluation. They interpreted that the requirement for citizen review could be satisfied by involving the center's board in reviewing the evaluation report. In addition, there seemed to be a common misconception that the required annual evaluation report is for federal consumption, not for use by the center or to inform residents of the center's catchment area. This report was usually judged by center staff to be of little use to the center; it was seldom nontechnical, brief, and educational enough to be useful to lay citizens.

When center staff and boards were asked what they recommended about the program evaluation requirements, the most popular choices were (a) to maintain the present guidelines with more clarification, technical assistance, and responsive monitoring or (b) to require a "core" of accountability data (such as use of services and costs) plus the annual conduct of the center's choice of a given number of other studies. Evaluators, administrators, and fiscal managers preferred the former; clinicians and "citizen" board members preferred the latter. Least desired was elimination of the program evaluation requirements.

Observations and Suggestions

Three observations seem to apply to the relations between echelons: (1) While centers have complained about details of the program evaluation requirements imposed on local centers by the federal government, they clearly approve of an evaluation requirement. Thus, local agencies recognize the need for a government standard-setting role. (2) While local agencies use discretion in their compliance with requirements, they also comply uncritically and inappropriately with some requirements, resulting in expenditure of scarce center resources on underutilized evaluation. Government, therefore, should apply requirements cautiously—preferably after field tests. This plea for legislators to be experiment-minded is not new. Perhaps the lesson for evaluators is to try to foresee and set up tests of program options before legislation is passed, rather than wait for legislators to decide what laws they favor. We often talk about feeding evaluation into planning. We should talk more about feeding planning into evaluation. (3) There should be a more realistic and effective division of labor in fact-finding between general variable-related research and program-related research. Bernstein and Freeman

(1975) argued that evaluation studies required both process and outcome assessments to learn how to change the program to improve its output. Outcome studies are expensive, especially when controls are used. Without controls results are misleading, usually overstating program achievements. This misinformation will not improve programs, but is useful in advocacy. Programs have little incentive to correct this bias, and are therefore easily led from careful studies to improve their programs to sloppy studies which aid in advocating the programs.

A solution to this paradox in program evaluation requires more extensive resources and concern for the broad public interest which are (or should be) more naturally accumulated at national or state government levels. Government funds should be used for research to establish the relation between service processes and outcomes as can only be done with careful experimental or analytic treatment controls, across a range of service process conditions and client problems and using a range of outcome criteria. Families of studies of this type, well controlled and well described, would enable local agencies to focus their program evaluation on achievement of service processes which research indicates leads to improved client outcome. For example, if we know from research how much a process such as continuity of care helps certain types of clients under various conditions, the program would need only to establish how much it provides continuity of care to know how much good that does for its clients.

We have a final suggestion which takes the form of a pretentious simile. There may be a developmental sequence to the functioning of program evaluators somewhat similar to the career of a meteor. First, the evaluator enters the atmosphere of program evaluation from a foreign background such as graduate school, academic research, or clinical practice. Second, on entering the atmosphere of program evaluation the evaluator burns with a rationalistic hope that program evaluation information will reform the world because managers want to learn how to improve their programs and will act on that information. The third developmental stage varies among three types. Some program evaluators burn out from cynicism caused by the political considerations in evaluation. Some evaluators pass through program evaluation, hurtling back into the "outer space" of academic research or clinical practice. A variant of this latter stage is when the evaluator is coopted by the program, turning the program evaluation endeavor into simple program support. The third alternative career is that some successful evaluators hit the "earth," causing a program impact.

NOTES

1. This analysis included five items of "other" activities under subheadings of classes of activities. A copy of the survey and the items used is available from the senior author.

2. Since this was an exploratory study, we did not rely on tests of statistical reliability. Chi-square tests of the proportions of centers claiming program changes from evaluations showed clusters 14 and 3 differing at the .05 level; but the difference between clusters 14 and 1 was quite likely to be due to chance (P > .30).

3. The Philadelphia Health Management Corporation studied only eight of the nine topics, excluding "availability."

REFERENCES

BASS, R. D. and C. WINDLE (1972) "Continuity of care: An approach to measurement." American Journal of Psychiatry 129:196-201.

BERNSTEIN, I. N. and H. E. FREEMAN (1975) Academic and Entrepreneurial Reserach: The Consequences of Diversity in Federal Evaluation Studies. New York: Russell Sage.

CHU, F. D. and S. TROTTER (1974) The Madness Establishment: Ralph Nader's Study Group Report on the National Institute of Mental Health. New York: Grossman.

HAGEDORN, H., K. J. BECK, S. F. NEUBERT, and S. H. WERLIN (1976) A Working Manual of Simple Program Evaluation Techniques for Community Mental Health Centers, DHEW Publication No. (ADM) 76-404. Washington, DC: U.S. Government Printing Office.

HARGREAVES, W. A., ATTKISSON, C. C. and J. E. SORENSEN (1977) Resource Materials for Community Mental Health Program Evaluation, DHEW Publication No. (ADM) 77-328, Washington, DC: U.S. Government Printing Office.

HARGREAVES, W. A., C. C. ATTKISSON, M. H. McINTYRE, and L. M. SIEGEL (1975) "Current applications of evalution." In J. Zusman and C. R. Wurster (eds.) Program Evaluation. Lexington, MA: D. C. Heath.

KATZ, J. (1977) "Cover-up and collective integrity: On the natural antagonisms of authority internal and external to organizations." Social Problems 25:3-17.

KIRESUK, T.J., S.H. LUND, S. K. SCHULTZ, and N. E. LARSEN (1977) "Change research at the Program Evaluation Resource Center." Evaluation 4:89-95.

McINTYRE, M. H., C. C. ATTKISSON and T. W. KELLER (1977) "Components of program evaluation capability in community mental health centers." In W. A. Hargreaves, C. C. Attkisson, and J. E. Sorensen (eds.) Resource Materials for Community Mental Health Program Evaluation, DHEW Publication No. (ADM) 77-328. Washington, DC: U.S. Government Printing Office.

MAJCHRZAK, A. and C. WINDLE (n.d.) "Patterns of program evolution in community mental health centers."

MONTAGUE, E. K. and E. N. TAYLOR (1971) Preliminary Handbook on Procedures for Evaluating Mental Health Indirect Service Programs in Schools. Alexandria, VA: Human Resources Research Organization.

NEIGHER, W. D. (forthcoming) Agency sponsored, federally funded program evaluation: The donkey and the cart.

Philadelphia Health Management Corporation (1978) A Review of Community Mentai Health Centers' Evaluation Activities: Phase One. Draft report to NIMH on Contract No. 278-77-0067 (MH), July.

REIDEL, D. C., G. L. TISCHLER, and J. K. MYERS (1974) Patient Care Evaluation in Mental Health Programs. Cambridge: Ballinger.

RISKA, E. and J. A. TAYLOR (1978) "Consumer attitudes toward health policy and knowledge about health legislation." Journal of Health Politics, Policy and Law 3: 112-123.

ROOS, N. P. (1974) "Influencing the health care system: Policy alternatives." Public Policy 22:139-167.

ROSEN, B. M., L. LAWRENCE, H. F. GOLDSMITH, C. D. WINDLE, and J. P. SHAMBAUGH (1975) Mental Health Demographic Profile System: Purpose, Contents, and Sampler of Uses, DHEW Publication No. (ADM) 76-263. Washington, DC: U.S. Government Printing Office.

SCHEIRER, M. A. (1978) "Program participants' positive perceptions: Psychological conflict of interest in social program evaluation." Evaluation Quarterly 2:53-70.

SCHICK, A. (1971) "From analysis to evaluation." The Annals 394:57-71.

SORENSEN, J. E. and D. S. PHIPPS (1972) Cost-Finding and Rate-Setting for Community Mental Health Centers. Association of Mental Health Administrators, DHEW Publication No. (HSM) 72-9138. Washington, DC: U.S. Government Printing Office.

STOCKDILL, J. W. and S. S. SHARFSTEIN (1976) "The politics of program evaluation: The mental health experience." Hospital and Community Psychiatry 27: 650-653.

U.S. General Accounting Office (1974) Need for More Effective Management of Community Mental Health Centers Program. Report to the Congress, B-164031(5). Washington, DC: U.S. Government Printing Office.

WEISS, C. H. (1975) "Evaluation research in the political context." In E. L. Stuening and M. Guttentag (eds.) Handbook of Evaluation Research (Vol. 1). Beverly Hills, CA: Sage.

——— (1970) "The politicization of evaluation research." Journal of Social Issues 26: 57-68.

WHOLEY, J. S., J. N. NAY, J. W. SCANLON, and R. E. SCHMIDT (1975) "Evaluation: When is it really needed?" Evaluation 2:89-93.

WINDLE, C. and P. BATES (1974) "Evaluating program evaluation: A suggested approach." In P. O. Davidson, F. W. Clark, and L. A. Hamerlynck (eds.) Evaluation of Behavioral Programs. Champaign, IL: Research Press.

WINDLE, C. and F. M. OCHBERG (1975) "Enhancing program evaluation in the Community Mental Health Centers Program." Evaluation 2:31-36.

WINDLE, C. and E. VOLKMAN (1973) "Evaluation in the Centers Program." Evaluation 1:69-70.

WINDLE, C., R. D. BASS, and C. A. TAUBE (1974) "PR aside: Initial results from NIMH's service program evaluation studies." American Journal of Community Psychology 2:311-327.

PART II

Policy-Making and Program Evaluation
in Specific Policy Areas

J. Richard Woy

National Institute of Mental Health

3

POLICY-MAKING FOR MENTAL HEALTH:
The Role of Program Evaluation

This essay is designed to examine the relationship between program evaluation and the development of policy in the mental health field. This discussion will concentrate on the national perspective: national policies in relation to community mental health. The chapter will also examine the role of program evaluation in relation to two national community mental health programs, both of them supported by the National Institute of Mental Health (NIMH).

Any analysis of national policies is particularly important because such policies are not always congruent with the policies of state and local government. Ours is a federal system of government, and responsibility for many governmental activities— including care for the mentally ill—is shared by all three levels of government. An extremely important element in the success of mental health programs is the degree to which policies and programs at different levels of government are *congruent* and *complementary*. A national policy may have limited impact if it runs counter to key policies at state and local levels. On the other

AUTHOR'S NOTE: *This chapter was presented as part of a panel entitled "The History, Results, and Impact of Policy-Oriented Evaluations" at the Evaluation Research Society Second Annual Meeting, November 2, 1978, Washington, D.C. The opinions expressed herein are those of the author and do not necessarily reflect the official policy of the National Institute of Mental Health.*

hand, very modest national programs can have enormous impact if they support and encourage certain state and local programs and policies.

Program evaluation will be discussed in relation to two NIMH-supported national community mental health programs. One of them is the Community Mental Health Centers (CMHC) program; the other is the Community Support Program (CSP). One is old; one is new. One is large; one is small. One has been studied and evaluated extensively; as yet the other has not been evaluated at all.

The stated purpose of the Community Mental Health Centers (CMHC) program is to make comprehensive community-based mental health care available to every resident of the United States. Begun in 1963, this program has sought its goal by providing project grants to initiate CMHCs. Grants to build or renovate facilities and grants to hire staff and pay other expenses have been provided. Each federally funded CMHC must provide a wide range of mental health services, including a variety of inpatient, ambulatory, and indirect services; each center is responsible for the mental health needs of a specific geographical area. As the federal "seed money" in each CMHC declines and then terminates over a period of eight years, each center is expected to find other sources of revenue, much of it from state and local government, to ensure its continued operation. The federal program is administered by the NIMH through ten regional offices across the country. There are approximately 700 operating CMHCs for the approximately 1500 possible catchment areas in the United States, and the FY 1978 appropriation for CMHCs was approximately $250 million.

Since 1969, the NIMH has conducted over 50 evaluation studies of the CMHC program at a cost of approximately $5 million. In addition, the Division of Biometry and Epidemiology of NIMH regularly collects and analyzes extensive and detailed information about CMHCs, and a number of other studies and analyses of the CMHC program have been conducted by non-government organizations. While the overall cost of these many studies is only a tiny fraction of the federal investment in the program, the CMHC program has been studied and analyzed much more intensively than any other component of the nation's mental health system and perhaps more than any other federal program of comparable size and importance.

While the stated purpose of the program sounds fairly simple and direct, in practice it encompasses a great variety of goals and purposes which are sometimes forced to compete with each other because of limited resources.

The purpose of the Community Support Program (CSP) is to demonstrate that the coordination and integration of currently fragmented human services can improve the level of functioning and well-being of seriously mentally disabled adults living outside institutions. This program, which is now only one year old and operating on a very modest budget, supports projects of two types in approximately 20 states. Half of the projects support state-wide planning for community support systems; others support development of actual community support systems in local areas. Three aspects of this new and highly visible program are particularly worth emphasizing. First, the program provides support for activities to integrate and coordinate already existing services, not to add additional services. Second, the program's basic concept extends well beyond the traditional boundaries of health services to include basic health and human services—including housing assistance, income maintenance, basic medical care, legal advocacy, vocational assistance, recreational and social services, and the like. Third, the program consciously is designed to make state governments the primary recipients of the funds and the primary actors in the development of such systems of care for the chronic mentally ill.

To date, of course, there are no completed evaluations of the CSP program. Planning for the first major national evaluative effort is near completion, and several other evaluation projects are in earlier stages of development.

FOUR BASIC LESSONS

It seems that four basic lessons can be drawn from the NIMH experience with evaluation of community mental health programs. Each stems from a variety of experiences and has fairly clear implications for the future.

First, for purposes of meaningful input into policy-making, the development and maintenance of good, routine ongoing data systems on NIMH programs as well as other mental health programs is extremely important. The availability of systematic quantitative information which provides an ongoing up-to-date description of the program is extremely useful in the policy context. Such information allows examination of trends over time, and data from such a system sometimes provide adequate information bearing on certain issues without the need for additional discrete studies. In addition, data from an ongoing system are always available for use, and delays engendered in conducting a new study are avoided. The most useful single evaluative tool for analysis of the CMHC program has been the yearly data from the *Annual Inventory of Community Mental Health Centers*. Virtually every major analysis and policy paper on the CMHC program has relied on descriptive information from the *Annual Inventory*, and data from the inventory have been analyzed and used in a variety of policy contexts. The most recent major report to make extensive use of data from this source is the broad assessment of the CMHC program which appeared in the *Report of the President's Commission on Mental Health* (1978). Analyses of the *Annual Inventory* have been useful in documenting the amounts of services rendered to clients, the characteristics of clients served by centers, the financial status of CMHCs, and a variety of other equally important issues.

As a result, the NIMH is attempting to upgrade and improve this capability. The *Annual Inventory* is a program-based rather than a client-based system, and so all of the data is collected in aggregate form. As a result, important analyses of client characteristics in relation to various aspects of the service system are not possible. During the past year the NIMH carried out a feasibility study for a large-scale, client-based panel survey of CMHCs, and during this year the institute plans to start implementation of such a survey in between 50 and 100 centers.

In addition, the first major national component of the evaluation of the CSP program will be a client-based data system which gathers data on sociodemographic characteristics, client functioning, and services received for each CSP client.

The *second major lesson* learned in attempts to apply results of program evaluation in the policy context is to confine evaluation studies to carefully delineated questions about discrete program areas or functions. CMHCs, like many other public programs, carry out a variety of functions and are concurrently pursuing a number of objectives. Any attempt to evaluation all of them at once is unrealistic and naive. In addition, attempts to carry out once-and-for-all, one-shot, all-or-nothing, yes-no evaluations of programs such as the CMHC program represent a basic misunderstanding of the policy-making process. For broad-aim social programs such as this one, policy evolves gradually over time as a result of a variety of inputs based on a variety of perspectives and varying interests in the program. No single evaluation study can hope to be definitive in such a context. What one group views as a strength, others may view as a weakness. What one interest group feels is crucial, others may view as irrelevant. In such a context, program evaluation results tend to add to the weight of evidence on one side or the other of many smaller policy questions about the program.

The extent to which and the manner in which results of program evaluation affect national policy are never entirely clear. A direct linear relationship between results of an evaluation study and a policy decision rarely exists. All of this notwithstanding, however, one can point to a number of instances in the distant and more recent past in which recommendations based upon results of clearly targeted program evaluation studies have suggested changes in policy, played a part in policy discussions, and ultimately have been implemented in the form of revised national policies.

(1) A study of NIMH programs on aging (Socio-Technical Systems, 1974) pointed out deficiencies in CMHCs' services to the elderly and recommended increased emphasis in this area. The CMHC Amendments of 1975 added the requirement that services specially designed for the elderly be a part of every CMHC.

(2) An evaluation of citizen participation in CMHCs (New et al., 1972) was very critical of this aspect of centers' operation, and specific provisions requiring representative citizen governing boards for CMHCs were included in Title III of P. L. 94-63.

(3) Evaluations of the adequacy of CMHCs' relationships with other human service agencies (Socio-Technical Systems, 1972) found fault with the centers' services to the chronically mentally ill and the relationships between CMHCs and state mental hospitals dealing with this patient group. Again, new sections were added to the CMHC Amendments of 1975 addressing this problem, and this study was a part of the environment which stimulated development of the CSP Program itself.

(4) An early study examined the "catchment area concept" (Little, 1973), which requires that each CMHC assume responsibility for the mental health of the residents of a defined geographical area. The study found the concept to be viable and a contributor to improved care, and the catchment area concept has been retained in all of the subsequent amendments to the CMHC act.

(5) A recent in-house study examined the experiences new CMHCs were having in implementing all twelve of the services mandated in the CMHC Amendments of 1975 (Eichler, 1978). Informal input from the field indicated that many CMHCs were having great difficulty implementing these requirements of the law. The in-house study confirmed these informal impressions, and the CMHC Bill passed in October 1978 simplified the requirements by reducing the required number of services from twelve to seven and giving greater flexibility to local communities for planning their CMHCs' services.

These are a few of the instances in which results of program evaluation studies targeted to specific program functions and goals have provided input into the policy-making process for the CMHC program.

As with the CMHC program, the development of a strategy for evaluation of the CSP program is being developed around a number of the program's key concepts and goals. Planning for evaluation studies is being carried out in the following areas to date: (1) the costs of CSP programs, (2) the impact of CSP upon the human service delivery system as it relates to the adult chronic mentally disabled, (3) an assessment of the population in need of this program nationwide, and (4) the relative impact of the CSP upon the functioning of its clients. Other projects focusing upon other questions will be developed in the future.

The *third major lesson* learned is that broad input into the planning of evaluation research and wide dissemination of results is desirable if evaluation is to play a meaningful role in policy-making. The participants in national mental health policy-making are numerous and varied, and each participant has a different perspective and carries out a different function in the process. Certain key subcommittees of the House of Represent-atives and Senate, the NIMH and other parts of DHEW, and a variety of national mental health interest groups—including the professional associations, state governments, hospitals and other service provider organizations, hospital unions, and health in-surance companies—tend to be the most active in this area. How-ever, occasionally, others, such as public interest and consumer organizations, the General Accounting Office (GAO), and the Office of Management and Budget (OMB) become involved. On some occasions, even the White House itself has been an active participant, as was the case with President Kennedy and, within the past two years, through Mrs. Carter's personal interest in mental health. Any or all of these players in the arena of national mental health policy-making may be interested in the results of program evaluation and may have suggestions for critical issues requiring evaluation.

Consequently, several things in the past couple of years have been done to increase both input into the planning of evaluation research and the development of improved dissemination. First, attempts have been made to develop formal liaisons with outside groups around issues of program evaluation. For over a year, the NIMH has met regularly with the Research and Evaluation Council of the National Council of CMHCs to discuss plans for NIMH evaluation research and to share information and im-prove systems to disseminate evaluation research findings. A similar arrangement with the Mental Health Liaison Group, which is made up of representatives of a variety of mental health interest groups, is now being initiated. Second, efforts have been made to put the results of past and recently completed NIMH evaluation research in a more readily usable form, and efforts were made to announce the presence of this information through a variety of forums, such as meetings of the Evaluation Research Society. The final reports of most NIMH evaluation studies are available from the National Technical Information Service. A glossary of the more than 100 studies is available from the Office of Program Development and Analysis, as are brief three- to five-page summaries of many completed studies. In addition, summaries of studies relevant to particular clusters of issues are being developed.

In the case of the CSP program, the process of developing the evaluation of that program has had extremely broad participation from a variety of quarters. The uniform data-collection project to be initiated shortly benefited from extensive involvement of the projects themselves, as well as the involvement of a variety of consultants and groups outside the government. Plans for the next steps in the evaluation of this new program will employ the same method.

The *final lesson learned* from the NIMH evaluation experience is the importance of keeping in mind the timing of program evaluation—in particular, the developmental nature of programs and the cyclical nature of decision-making. Perhaps the point here is made best by the following lines from *Ecclesiastes,* Chapter 3, Verses 1 through 3:

> To every thing there is a season, and a time to every purpose under the heaven:
>
> A time to be born, and a time to die; a time to plant, and time to pluck up that which is planted;
>
> A time to kill, and a time to heal; a time to break down, and a time to build up.

If program evaluation is to have meaningful input into policy development, it must provide answers to the right questions at the right time.

One factor to keep in mind in terms of timing is the stage of development of the program. Depending upon whether a program is just getting started, partially developed, mature, or in decline, the nature of the policy questions will vary, and evaluation studies focused upon questions relevant to other stages will be either too late to be useful or else will have to wait to be utilized. A series of studies done at different points in the life of the CMHC program on the "seed money" concept illustrates this point. The efficacy of the seed money concept is a cornerstone of the CMHC program because the future of community mental health programs depends upon continued funding after their time-limited grant funding expires.

Earlier studies of the funding of CMHCs focused upon the adequacy of centers' preparations for the end of federal grant funding, and made recommendations designed to help assure an adequate transition to other sources of revenue. Now that a significant number of CMHCs have completed their period of federal funding, recent studies have examined the effects of termination of federal funds on CMHCs and have offered recommendations designed to help some centers that are encountering difficulties.

Another important factor to keep in mind in terms of the timing of program evaluation studies is the cyclical nature of decision-making. The CMHC legislation has been amended a number of times since its original passage in 1963, and all of the amendments, including the current one, have been time limited. Evaluation studies designed to provide input into legislation and in turn the development of regulations and guidelines must be completed in time to fit into the schedule determined by the legislative process.

SUMMARY

This chapter has attempted to draw some lessons from the NIMH's experience in attempting to use the results of program evaluation in the context of national policy-making for mental health. Four important lessons can be learned from that experience. First, routine reporting systems are extremely useful in the policy context because the ongoing quantitative picture of programs which they provide is an extremely flexible and powerful tool for analysis of issues in a variety of policy areas. Second, the importance of clearly delineating the specific issues and questions to be addressed cannot be overemphasized. Results will be useful only if the questions are manageable and clear. Third, because there are a variety of individuals and groups involved in the national policy-making arena for mental health—all of whom are current or potential users of evaluation results—the desirability of broad input into the evaluation planning process and wide dissemination of results is extremely important. Finally, the NIMH experience indicates that for results of program evaluation to be useful in the policy context, they must be available at certain crucial times in the legislative and policy development process. These several lessons gleaned from past NIMH efforts to evaluate its programs provide some direction for future activities in this area.

REFERENCES

Task Panel on Community Mental Health Centers Assessment (1978) "Report of the Task Panel on Community Mental Health Centers Assessment." In Task Panel Reports, Submitted to the President's Commission on Mental Health (Vol. II). Washington, DC: U.S. Government Printing Office.

Socio-Technical Systems, Inc. (1974) Evaluation of NIMH Aging Programs with Special Focus on Services. Report to NIMH on Contract No. HSM-42-72-197, Accession No. PB-247-183. Springfield, VA: National Technical Information Service.

NEW, P. K., W. E. HOLTON, and R. M. HESSLER (1972) Citizen-Participation and Interagency Relations: Issues and Program Implications for CMHCs. Report to NIMH on Contract No. HSM-42-70-99, Accession No. PB-210-093. Springfield, VA: National Technical Information Service.

Socio-Technical Systems, Inc. (1972) Study of the Relationship between CMHCs and State Mental Hospitals. Report to NIMH on Contract No. HSM-42-70-107, Accession No. PB-249-485. Springfield, VA: National Technical Information Service.

Arthur D. Little, Inc. (1973) Viability of the Catchment Area Concept. Report to NIMH on Contract No. HSM-42-72-96, Accession No. PB-225-703. Springfield, VA: National Technical Information Service.

EICHLER, A. (1978) The Community Mental Health Centers Amendments of 1975: (Title III of P. L. 94-63): How are the New CMHCs Doing? Rockville, MD: National Institute of Mental Health.

Michael Radnor
H. Durward Hofler
Northwestern University

4

BEYOND MEASUREMENT TO APPROPRIATENESS AND LEARNING
Evaluating LEAA Experimental Programs

Evaluation research is carried out and supported to provide policy makers and program managers with help on their ongoing and future program/project activities. This help may be in terms of evaluating whether or not a specific program has been more or less successful. Essentially, this is done by measuring the program outcomes against certain goal statements, as were used to initiate the program and/or as modified. This is the most common perspective used in evaluation research used by those teaching and practicing the subject. While there are certainly benefits to be obtained for policy makers from such approaches, we believe that, standing alone, these are frequently insufficient and have serious defects which strongly undermine validity and usefulness.

The problems arise for a number of reasons, which will be discussed in this article. Briefly, we would argue that these problems are related to the following:

(1) *Goals structure.* Deciding what are or what should be the goals of a program is far from a trivial exercise. Programs or projects

AUTHORS' NOTE: *This chapter was originally prepared for the Evaluation Research Society Second Annual Meeting, November 1-4, 1978, L'Enfant Plaza Hotel, Washington, D.C. The authors wish to thank Andrew Weiss for his valuable comments and assistance.*

often "fail," not because they did not achieve what they set out to achieve or even what the program managers hoped they would achieve, but because they were inappropriate to the situation, at any time or as the context changed, and/or because the process by which they were set was inappropriate. Further, it can be very dangerous to consider the goals of an individual program apart from the goals of other (past, present, or future) programs in the same policy domain.

(2) *The cumulativeness of programs and knowledge.* What an agency does or knows is not based on a series of isolated efforts or studies—it builds cumulatively over time. Therefore, programs must also be viewed in terms of their additive (or subtractive) or direction-changing character over time. There are also important ongoing *portfolio* characteristics to be considered. A program standing alone may (or may not) contribute in how it relates (synergistically or competitively) to other current and projected programs. This is a common consideration in selecting programs for R & D portfolios or products for a line.

(3) The nature of the *context* in which programs are designed, implemented, and maintained is critical to appreciating what needs to be done at a programmatic level. Further, it is to be recognized that evaluations are called for in situations where some innovation has been introduced. Innovation carries with it all the uncertainties that become involved in introducing and managing change. Hence, it becomes of critical importance for the evaluator to have a well-grounded *theory of the phenomenon* with respect to the process of change, the innovation, and the context involved.

(4) Programs reflect *intraorganizational and interorganizational realities* (of decision and power structures, information flows, and the like) as well as the problems they are designed to ameliorate. It is also important to know how to factor in consideration of such constraints and pressures—we also need a theory of the decision/information processes that relate to the programs, portfolios, operating practices, and so on.

These issues lead us to consider a second potential (and, in the long run, perhaps more important) benefit from evaluation research, one that we feel has been neglected to date: helping policy makers understand what effects they are causing and why it is they do what they do, and even more specifically, why they seem to continue making the same mistakes over and over again (despite the results of the evaluation studies). This perspective recognizes that policy and program evaluation may be most useful when it helps policy/decision makers to help themselves by helping them better understanding their decision-making processes and context. Thus, we suggest that another critical and relatively neglected function of evaluation research is to aid in the process of *organizational learning* by providing to policy makers information as to how programs measure up to these objectives.

We are further suggesting that evaluation research needs to be based on an understanding of (1) the interaction among goals, context, and theory; (2) the nature of program development as an ongoing, interactive, and cumulative process; and (3) the nature of the process of innovation.

We recognize that the above suggestions may not provide what a policy maker asks of an evaluation researcher. Nonetheless, it is our view that for evaluation research to be useful for either policy makers or for researchers, these are issues which must be addressed. We believe that lack of attention to these issues has been a major reason for the limited impact of evaluation research to date.

SCENARIOS FOR EVALUATION RESEARCH

It may be helpful at this point to pose two brief scenarios which may highlight the above considerations. The first scenario, though posed hypothetically, is abstracted from an actual case of evaluation research which we will discuss later in this chapter. The second scenario is purely hypothetical and admittedly oversimplified, but serves the purpose of setting the process of evaluation in a policy context. Both scenarios make explicit two critical questions: What is the function of evaluation research —what is it supposed to tell us? What factors should be considered during the process of evaluation research?

Scenario 1. A federal agency whose area of concern is in a social service sector comes to the conclusion that a particular technological device being used in that sector is not adequate.

The agency therefore prepares a Request for Proposals (RFP) for an improved device. Specifications are set concerning the size, capabilities, and productions costs for the improved device. Two years are allowed for development of the device; thus, two years later, a new product has been developed which meets the above-stated specifications. At this time an evaluation is performed on this program.

Question: What would be the nature, conclusions, and recommendations of evaluation research?

Scenario 2. Now let us set a somewhat different scene. We now have a newly appointed director of a federal agency. In a meeting of the director and division heads of the agency, the following discussion occurs.

Director: In reviewing the operation of the agency, I note that Congress has mandated that our programs be evaluated. How is this being done?

Division Head: Whenever we develop a program, we hire an external evaluation research firm to evaluate the program.

Director: Why is this evaluation research considered so important? What is it supposed to tell us?

Division Head: It tells us whether a particular program has obtained its objectives.

Director: How have we been doing?

Division Head: Well, according to the evaluation research reports, most of our programs have come pretty close to meeting targeted goals. A few haven't.

Director: Sounds like most of our personnel know how to run a program. Now here are some programs I think we need to develop. Of course, we'll have to cut back in some of the existing programs to make room for these. I think these program changes are responsive to the criticism this agency has been getting from Congress lately.

BROADENING THE PERSPECTIVE
ON EVALUATION RESEARCH

The above discussion suggests that evaluation research may have two different kinds of focal concerns. On the one hand would be an inward-oriented focus which limits itself to a single program and focuses on the program per se. In this case, evaluation research would be concerned primarily with assessing program goals in terms of the clarity and measurability and in terms of their attainment; it also may be concerned with the implementation of the program in terms of the adequacy of the implementation plan and in terms of whether it was implemented in the ways intended.

On the other hand, another type of evaluation would be an outward-oriented focus that looks beyond the program itself to the context in which the program is embedded. Such outwardly focused evaluation research would be concerned both with the external environment in which the program is implemented and with the internal context of the agency which has developed the program (in terms of other agency programs and in terms of the agency's policy-making structures and processes).

We are not, of course, suggesting that these two types of focal concerns can or should be separated or that one is more important than the other. Quite to the contrary, we are suggesting that they are highly interactive and that either focus apart from the other becomes trivialized. We are, however, concerned that evaluation research today has tended to overemphasize an inward-oriented focus on the program itself.

The Current Perspective of Evaluation Research—
An Inward Orientation

As currently taught and applied, evaluation research focuses inwardly on a specific program rather than on the context in which the program is embedded. As noted by our hypothetical division head, the primary concern of evaluation research has been to determine whether or not a specific program has obtained specified goals—that is, on whether or not it has "succeeded" or "failed." Attention also may be given to implementation of the program (adequacy of the implementation plan; whether the program was implemented in the prescribed manner) and to the basic cause-effect theory underlying the program design (whether X does indeed cause Y, or whether some other X is more powerful). As a result of this perspective, concerns about evaluation research designs have focused on (1) ensuring the clarity and measurability of stated goals and (2) indicators of and the methodology for measuring attainment of stated goals.

The Use of Evaluation Research

This description of the current use of evaluation is enticing. On the surface it seems to make sense: It is straight-forward; based upon a well-accepted view of the scientific method; focuses upon a coherent unit of analysis (a single program); *and* it is bottom-line, results oriented (a significant consideration for government policy makers who must justify their funding requests).

Three questions, however, give rise to serious doubt about the usefulness—and validity—of evaluation research as currently taught and applied:

(1) Given the vast amount of evaluation research over the past decade, why is it that agencies and their policy makers continue to make the "same mistakes?"
(2) Why are findings of evaluation research in the social sciences so unstable and contradictory?
(3) What happens if (as is often the case in the social science/service arena) "bottom line" results are "muddy?"

These questions suggest a critical need to reexamine the nature and purpose of evaluation research in terms of the two critical questions posed earlier: (1) What is evaluation research supposed to tell us? and (2) What factors must be considered during the process of evaluation research? We suggest that, as currently applied, evaluation research has not been—nor can it be—as useful as it needs to be for either policy makers or researchers precisely because it has focused too narrowly on and assumed too much about outcomes and stated goals of a single program.

Going Beyond Measurement to Appropriateness—
The Intertwining of Goals, Context, and Theory

We recognize, of course, the importance of measuring goal attainment—and therefore the importance of clearly stated goals and of the indicators and methodology used to measure goal attainment. However, the measurement of goal attainment per se —no matter how clearly stated and measurable the goals may be—does not deal with a very critical issue: the *appropriateness* of the goals. Yet it is hard to understand how it would be helpful for a policy maker to know that a program had attained its stated goals if it is not clear whether or not the goal was appropriate in the first place. Indeed, at worst, this could lead to the continuance of dysfunctional goals.

The question arises as to how one defines or determines the appropriateness of a program and its goal, and this question may be answered from several perspectives. Appropriateness may be defined in relation to the legislated purpose and mission of an agency. Appropriateness also may be defined in relation to the other programs of an agency.

Our concern here is the appropriateness of a program in relation to the context in which it is implemented. From this perspective, it is not difficult to illustrate how a program evaluated on the basis of goal attainment may lead one to give the right answer to the wrong question.

For example, a program with the goal of developing a specific technology (as in our first scenario) may succeed in doing so. However, such a goal might be inappropriate under several conditions: (a) if there are inadequate linkages for dissemination and diffusion of the technology; (b) if the technology would require large capital investment by firms which only recently have made long-term capital investments in a technology which serves the same basic function; (c) if potential users of the technology lack adequate technical expertise and do not have access to technical assistance; or (d) if regulations of governmental agencies would effectively prevent the acquisition and use of the technology as developed in the program. In each of these situations, the successfully developed technology would be useless for all practical purposes—it would literally "sit on the shelf." How, then, could such a program really be deemed "successful?"

These illustrations indicate how context interacts with program goals in ways that are significant to policy makers above and beyond the attainment of program goals. They illustrate how a program may be addressing the wrong issue, or where there is a need for prior or complementary programs.

For another example, we must consider how changes in the context may be affecting the phenomenon being evaluated. A program goal might be appropriate at one point in time (such as when initial decisions were made to develop the program) and yet be inappropriate at a later time because of changes in the context. This would be especially true for programs which require long periods of time for development and/or for implementation and goal attainment, or for programs which are intended for usage over extended periods of time. Thus, if evaluation largely ignores changes in the context of the program, it is once again difficult to see how a meaningful evaluation can be carried out and findings interpreted.

Another critical issue of appropriateness involves consideration of intended versus actual scope of a program. The stated program goal would, quite properly, state the *specific target* at which the program was aimed and the kind and level of *intended impact*. However, it would also seem important for an evaluation to ask whether or not the program is impacting *other* targets (and with what effects) and whether there are *unintended* kinds or levels of impact. Here, too, one would have to consider the nature of the context when evaluating the appropriateness of a program whose actual scope of targets and types of impacts are greater than intended.

The above discussion also points to another important consideration for evaluation research: the need to evaluate the theory underlying the program. We may properly assume that a program has been based on some theoretical assumptions or beliefs that certain kinds of actions lead to certain kinds of outcomes. Questions now arise concerning such matters as (1) whether the underlying assumptions have been explicitly and clearly explicated by the policy makers—or if perhaps the program is based on a sort of "hodgepodge" of "hit or miss" assumptions; (2) whether the underlying theory has adequately or appropriately specified the contextual condition under which the program could or could not succeed; (3) whether consideration had been given to the scope issues noted above; and (4) whether the assumed cause-effect relationship of program design to program goals is indeed tenable.

Going Beyond a Single Program to the Nesting of Programs

When an agency funds the evaluation of a specific program, it is axiomatic that the evaluation must focus on the details of that specific program. At the same time, we suggest that it is a critical mistake to evaluate that program apart from an understanding of the way it nests into other programs of the agency. The development of programs is not a series of disconnected, discrete events, but is an ongoing, interactive, and cumulative process over time. The way a particular program nests into the total set of programs of the agency can be seen from three perspectives.

The first perspective is that of *program portfolios*. This concept suggests consideration of such questions as: Does the program being evaluated complement or conflict with other agency programs in terms of goals, allocation of resources, or issues of timing? Is the program unnecessarily redundant? Is this a case where the program by itself failed, but could succeed if the agency were also to develop another, complementary program?

A second perspective is that of *balance across the various functional responsibilities of an agency*. In this case it would be important to ask such questions as whether the program being evaluated required such a high proportion of the agency's funds or personnel that the agency has had to neglect other important areas of its responsibility.

A third perspective would be *a longitudinal perspective which takes into consideration how programs interact over time in an ongoing, cumulative manner*. Thus, the total set of an agency's programs will have a set of characteristics such as mix and balance, emphases, and requirements on agency personnel and financial resources. These characteristics are developed and modified over time in a cumulative manner as new programs are developed and existing programs modified or dropped. Thus, the usefulness of an evaluation to a policy maker would be increased if the evaluation (of a single program) takes into consideration how the program does or is likely to affect the characteristics of the total set of agency programs, both currently and over time.

The above discussion has focused on the ongoing, cumulative nature of program development. It is also important to realize that these same observations apply to the user organizations for which a program has been developed. The effect of a program cannot be properly understood apart from the way the program nests into the total set of programs and activities of the user organization.

Going Beyond Programs to
Policy-Making Processes and Structures

Throughout this chapter we have been suggesting an increasingly expanding scope of factors to be considered in the process of evaluation research. We have suggested that evaluation research go beyond focusing on a single program and its goals to consideration of the context and of other agency programs. We are now suggesting that our scope of consideration go beyond programs to the structure and process of policy-making which lead to (and thus affect the nature of) decisions to develop a program.

At the beginning of this chapter we suggested that a basic purpose of evaluation research is to aid organizational learning in a way that would enable policy makers to avoid "making the same old mistakes." From this perspective, one must pose the question: How did we get into the position of developing a program that has failed, or of developing a program that attained its goals but was inappropriate? To ask this kind of question is to ask about the policy-making structure and process of the agency. It is to suggest that *how decisions are made* to develop programs or to develop them in a certain way or with certain goals may be at the root of the success, failure, or appropriateness of a program.

We are not suggesting that each and every program evaluation must involve a full-blown study and analysis of the policy-making structures and processes of an agency. We *are* suggesting that it *is* appropriate for an evaluation to point to the impact of the agency's policy-making processes on the success, failure, or appropriateness of a program being evaluated—*and* to suggest the implications thereof for future programs.

Including Consideration of the Nature of Innovation

Evaluations are generally requested in situations which call for innovation in some form or another. The characteristics of the process of innovation can affect the nature of the program development process; the final outcome of program development; and the dissemination, acquisition, and implementation/utilization of program outcomes. Thus, an evaluation would need to ask such questions as whether or not the program design and goal statements have adequately taken into consideration the nature and amount of uncertainty involved; the nature of the knowledge, personnel, and institutional bases; and the history of intended users with innovation in general and with this type of innovation in particular. Considerations such as these would lead the evaluation researcher to examine the feasibility as well as the attainment of goals, the appropriateness of the program design, and even the appropriateness of the policy decision to develop a program.

AN ILLUSTRATIVE CASE STUDY

We can now illustrate the significance of the above discussion in an actual case of evaluation research. The first scenario described at the beginning of this chapter is not hypothetical; it was drawn from an evaluation the authors were asked to provide in 1974 concerning the Equipment Systems Improvement Program (ESIP) of LEAA's National Institute of Law Enforcement and Criminal Justice.

On the surface, the ESIP program appeared reasonable: the program was premised on LEAA's judgment that (1) existing law

enforcement equipment did not reflect state-of-the-art technology, (2) state-of-the-art technology could be developed, and
that (3) such innovative technology would significantly improve
effectiveness and efficiency in the practice of law enforcement.
The program established for the development of innovative technology would not appear unreasonable:

(a) MITRE Corporation was contacted to provide a user needs
study—the premise being that technology development should
be based on needs.

(b) The National Bureau of Standards (NBS) was contacted to
develop equipment standards for both existing and new equipment—the premise being that the existence of standards would
encourage the use of better products and drive out inferior
products.

(c) Aerospace Corporation was contacted to manage and let contracts for development work on new technologies—the premise
being to use professional developers to guide and oversee the
development work.

The question now becomes: What were the results of this program and how should this program be evaluated?

From the perspective of evaluation research as currently
taught and applied, one might well have given high marks to
this program—or at least some specific elements of this program.
MITRE was highly criticized for its user needs analysis (though
one might question whether they were given a feasible task).
NBS met its stated objectives by developing highly professional
standards; Aerospace did a competent job of managing development work; and a number of innovative products were developed
that met the programs state-of-the-art specifications (Martin-
Marietta developed a hand-held, two-way radio that met LEAA's
program specifications as to size, weight, capability—the new
technological device described earlier in our "hypothetical"
scenario).

In terms of practical reality, however, one would have to
judge the ESIP program to be a failure. While a few products
were successfully developed, most did not impact practice or

the marketplace. For the most part, neither the ESIP program nor its products were popular with law enforcement agencies; the program was ultimately dropped.

The question now becomes: Why did a seemingly reasonable program which met many of its specified objectives fail? What can be learned from this program? How can evaluation research contribute to answering these first two questions?

We are suggesting that as long as evaluation research looks at programs separately and only in terms of specified goals and outcomes, these questions cannot be usefully answered. Rather, evaluation research must examine the interaction of goals and context. For example, in the law enforcement context, consideration must be given to such matters as:

(1) *The level professionalism of law enforcement with respect to specific types of equipment.* Law enforcement agencies vary considerably in size and, relatedly, in the technical capabilities of their personnel. Similarly, they have different types of equipment levels of technical sophistication; thus, for example, in matters of ballistics and firearms, police agencies either possess or have access to adequate technical expertise. On the other hand with the exception of the few largest cities, local police departments generally do not have personnel with high levels of technical sophistication in most areas, including two-way communication and night-vision equipment. This contextual reality helps to explain the failure of the NBS standards program noted above. While the NBS standards must be judged technically well developed, they were developed (written) at a level of technical sophistication appropriate for manufacturers (who neither needed nor wanted them) but quite inappropriate for most local police agencies (who could not use them, no matter how good the standards were). Thus, it is not surprising that local law enforcement agencies did not find the NBS standards more useful.

(2) *The funding problems of law enforcement agencies.* Local law enforcement agencies vary as to whether their budgets are tight (which most are) or not, though we found that most perceived their budgets to be tight (five years before Proposition 13). Further, around 90 percent of the typical agency's budget is

allocated to personal and administrative expenses—not to equipment acquisition. Further, of the remaining approximately 10 percent, by far the lion's share is allocated for such basics as vehicles and maintenance. In a word, the typical law enforcement agency has very little funding which it could,if it wanted to, allocate to the acquisition of innovative equipment.

(3) *The priorities of law enforcement agencies.* In setting a priority goal of developing innovative equipment, LEAA ran counter to law enforcement priorities held by local agencies.

(4) *The changing view toward equipment.* Over the last 10 to 20 years society has increasingly come to raise questions about the nature and use of law enforcement equipment. Further, questions can, should, and have been raised about a focus on equipment per se—that the prior question is the function which equipment might perform and whether acquiring or modifying equipment is the most appropriate way to perform the function in question.

(5) *The view of equipment producers about the law enforcement market.* In our study of the ESIP program we found a number of producers who were the primary sources of equipment for law enforcement agencies, but for whom law enforcement was only a secondary market. We further found producers who avoided the law enforcement market because of its fragmentation and the hassle involved in making bids, meeting requirements, and even getting paid.

(6) *The producer/user relation,* which in many cases exists under conditions of high dependency, but which are too often poorly institutionalized—with users lacking needed service and assistance.

We can illustrate the importance of contextual realities such as these—both for a program and for evaluation research—by describing the development of a hand-held, two-way radio by Martin Marietta Corporation under an ESIP program contract. LEAA believed that because Motorola held a dominant share of the two-way radio market in law enforcement, innovation was being held back. LEAA reasoned that by funding the independent development of a smaller, lighter, cheaper hand-held, two-way radio with improved capabilities, local law enforcement agencies would indeed purchase the improved equipment.

Viewed solely from the perspective of attainment of specified objectives (to develop a two-way radio at specified levels of size, capabilities, and so on), this program would have to be evaluated as successful—the improved equipment was, in fact, developed by Martin Marietta. However, Martin Marietta refused to produce and sell the radio unless the government could provide some form of subsidization. The radio, as a result, never entered the law enforcement market.

The point to be made here is that for evaluation research to be useful it must consider goal appropriateness and goal/context interaction and must not limit itself to measurement of goal attainment. In this case the program goal was to develop the product. This goal was attained, but it was an inappropriate goal given the realities of the law enforcement context. Specifically, it did not take into consideration: (1) that most law enforcement agencies lacked the level of technical capability needed to acquire and maintain the equipment; (2) that local law enforcement agencies were therefore dependent on technical assistance provided by the manufacturer; (3) that Motorola already had in place a nationwide sales-service network; and (4) that such a network wuld be very costly to develop and maintain.

Thus, in this case, evaluation research would need to focus not only on goal outcomes, but also on goal appropriateness in the light of contextual realities. From this latter perspective, the findings of evaluation research would point in the direction of suggesting that LEAA was working on the wrong *aspect* or *phase* of the problem. That is, a prior need would have been to upgrade the skills of technical assistance services available to local agencies. Then—and only then—would it be appropriate to encourage other firms to enter the law enforcement two-way radio market.

CONCLUSION

While recognizing that the evaluation of goal attainment of a specific program is valid and important (and therefore to be continued), the perspective and concern of evaluation research must be broadened to enable evaluation research to be useful to policy makers both in the short term and in the long term.

It is now important to take note of the critical role of policy makers in developing such a perspective. They are the ones who are most affected, and they are the ones who ask for evaluations. If anything, then, the emphasis of this chapter is the need for a proper understanding of the nature and function of evaluation research to be made an integral part of an agency's policy-making process. Indeed, the way an agency frames the questions and issues for evaluation would have a strong impact on the direction that evaluation research will take in the future. We also suggest that consideration of what kind of *evaluation* questions are to be posed also would likely have a beneficial effect on how a program is *designed.*

It is also important to examine the role that can be played by evaluation researchers. It is recognized, of course, that the agency—not the evaluation researcher—controls the final decision about an evaluation. Nonetheless, at the time an evaluation is being contracted, the evaluation researchers have both an opportunity and a responsibility to pose the issues of what function an evaluation can and should serve, how it can be most helpful to the policy maker, and what factors must be considered if the evaluation is to be useful. Further, as evaluations are performed, the evaluation researcher should be sensitive to issues of context, goal appropriateness, policy decision processes, and the like and—where appropriate—call these to the attention of policy makers either during the evaluation or in the reporting of evaluation findings and recommendations. If evaluation researchers do not take this initiative and responsibility, they would only be helping to perpetuate a limited usefulness of evaluation research and thereby creating problems with which they must ultimately deal.

Robert F. Rich
*Woodrow Wilson School of Public
and International Affairs,
Princeton University*

5

PROBLEM-SOLVING AND
EVALUATION RESEARCH
Unemployment Insurance Policy

Throughout modern western history, "expertise" has been recognized as the foundation of *power* and *legitimacy* for bureaucratic organizations. This "expertise" is derived from the technical skills individuals acquire from formal training/education, as well as the information/data individuals (civil servants) obtain and generate in connection with their official duties. Bureaucrats can be seen as experts who deal in a scarce commodity: knowledge. Weber equated bureaucratic expertise with knowledge, including both technical and substantive information relating to the organization's "sphere of interest." The possession of this expertise served as the foundation of bureaucratic power— bureaucrats were viewed as possessing greater *substantive* and *technical* expertise than other government officials; thus, as an organization, bureaucracy was viewed as being superior to all other governmental units. The bureaucratic organization has a comparative advantage: the possession of knowledge.

Presumably, according to organizational theory, this expertise (knowledge) will be used to guide official governmental policy-making. Politicians will benefit from the knowledge which is available to them through the bureaucracy. In the United States, the importance of knowledge for guiding policy-making dates back to the work of James Madison. Madison points out that the ideal state of affairs is one in which "knowledge will forever

govern ignorance; and a people who mean to be their own governors must arm themselves with the power which knowledge
gives." Madison's statement implicitly assumes that in processing
information bureaucrats will be most concerned with differentiat-
ing between relevant and irrelevant information and in helping
to improve the overall quality of decision making (Morss and
Rich, 1979).

This theoretical description of bureaucratic expertise is consistent with the traditional view of public administration first
developed by Weber: politics is separate from administration.
The role of the administrator/expert is to be guided by the goals
specified by the political leaders. The administrator—hence, the
government organization—is not supposed to have "interests" or
"goals" of its own.

As history has illustrated, the theoretical construct does not
reflect reality in modern industrialized states. Agencies develop
their own "organizational interests" independently from those
of the political leaders/executives. In most countries bureau-
cracies develop an ideology emphasizing their own autonomy
(Eisenstadt, 1969). A bureaucracy's preoccupation with maintaining and furthering the "organizational interests" is not
ncessarily synonymous with using knowledge/expertise in a
manner that is consistent with the Madisonian conception.

Indeed, in the United States, bureaucratic structures have
moved away from this ideal:

> [B]ut events were conspiring against the ideal. As society grew
> more complex, government grew more powerful. The instinct of
> bureaucracy, as Max Weber pointed out was to "increase the
> superiority of the professionally informed by keeping their knowl-
> edge and intentions secret." The concept of "official secret" was
> "the specific invention of bureaucracy" and officials defended
> nothing so emphatically as their secrets. Involvement in foreign
> affairs strengthened the addiction [Schlesinger, 1973].

Thus, the ideal of knowledge governing ignorance (enlightenment) was replaced by knowledge serving as the instrument for
obtaining and maintaining bureaucratic power.

The bureaucracy's position of power depends on the reliance of others (individuals in organizations) on their "expertise/knowledge." This suggests that the monopoly on the control and ownership of information is the key to the security of the bureaucracy agency. When viewed from this perspective, information/knowledge becomes a *political resource*. As Warren Illchman and Norman Upholff (1971) point out:

> The importance of secrecy in politics and government becomes clear when we understand information as a resource. The value of a particular piece of information is crucially affected by whether or not the possessor of that information has a monopoly. Once certain information is shared, its original owner experiences sharp decreases in control over its use. This is why secrets are only shared with persons with whom the original owner can exercise effective sanctions. Fear of such sanctions reduces the likelihood of further divulsion [sic] to others. The wider the distribution of information, however, the more cheaply information can be acquired. A monopoly owner of certain information can bargain to get a price approximating the full worth of that information to the purchaser, but when many people have the same information, each may be eager to get what he can before another does the same. The price paid must, however, exceed whatever losses can be suffered by the divulging person as a result as sanctions exercised by the original possessor.

The tendencies to seek monopolies is a natural outgrowth of concern over secrecy and fear of how others might use information, if it were to be shared with them.

INSULARITY AND REJECTION OF EXTERNAL SOURCES OF INFORMATION

This tendency for monopolistic control over the acquisition and utilization of information is consistent with a reliance of bureaucrats on their own expertise, a rejection of counterintuitive information, and a rejection of externally generated sources of information (external to the organization in question).

On the whole, bureaucrats and decision makers are hired on the basis of their expertise of knowledge in a given field. To a great extent their credibility, prestige, and legitimacy are related to the reliance of others on their knowledge. Many decision makers are reluctant to collect or contract information outside their agency or even from a different department within their own agency. Individual decision makers appear to feel more comfortable with the traditional channels they are familiar with, and whose values they can assess, than with an agency or individual with whom they have had little or no experience and for whom the decision maker has no basis to make a judgment concerning reliability of the information provided. Most officials seem to feel that conventional political channels are sufficient to yield the information desired or deemed necessary on policy grounds.

In some cases, there is a simple rejection of new information resources. Decision makers are under pressure to reduce the number of data sources they use. Once the investment has been made for information and an information channel is acquired, it is seen as "cheaper" to keep using it than to invest in new channels (Arrow, 1974).

It is also clearly the case that officials defer to expertise in the expectation that they will be likewise deferred to in what is considered their specialty. "To challenge the expertise of another career official is to risk retaliation." Most bureaucrats are extremely reluctant to challenge the stated views of those outside their substantive areas of concern.

This discussion of the development of organizational interests produces a clear picture of the role of knowledge/expertise in the day-to-day operation of bureaucratic operation:

(1) Knowledge is essential to the power and prestige of bureaucratic organization.
(2) Bureaucrats seek to promote this position.
(3) The desire to protect organizational interests is manifested in the tendency to hard information. Information/data is not shared among agencies, and often it is not shared across organizational units within the same agency. Indeed, there is evidence from a recent empirical study to show that there is resistance to sharing among bureaus or divisions within the same agency (Rich, 1979b).

(4) There is also a tendency not to collect new information—to rely on information already used within the organization. External uses of information are viewed with some suspicion.

(5) While it is certainly true that experts also have the right to seek information that is relevant to a problem under study, the "right" does not mean that others in government will readily volunteer to give information. The information is often not shared among/ between government officials.

ALTERNATIVE MODEL:
THE MODERN POLICY ANALYST

This model of the relationship between expertise and bureaucratic power is time bound; it stems from a time when official training for government service could produce individuals who were thoroughly knowledgeable in substantive areas. In addition, they possessed the technical skills necessary to continue to "stay on top of the field." Thus, training for the civil service emphasized substantive knowledge.

In modern times, substantive training has been assigned a much lower priority. It is no longer realistic to expect graduates to be thoroughly knowledgeable in a substantive area; training for a civil service position reflects this reality. *Methods* and *tools* of analysis are emphasized, along with thorough training on how to acquire the knowledge that is needed to keep abreast of substantive information/data that increases from year to year. Schools of public administration/public policy believe they are producing *analysts* who appreciate the value of "policy role of research," who are knowledgeable about external information sources that can provide up-to-date information, and who are familiar with the techniques/tools of analysis used by most policy researchers.

Individuals learn about the realities of scientific communication. Researchers/scholars remain abreast of new developments by being part of an "invisible college" of colleagues. When faced with a problem, individuals contact a colleague who is able to inform them of the most up-to-date information or give the name of another individual who has this information. Thus, through a series of phone calls, exchange of letters, and/or participation in professional meetings individuals in a particular network are aware of "the most current developments."

It will be fair to conclude that these individuals are socialized in the tradition of Madison's ideal: "People who mean to be their own governors must arm themselves with the power that knowledge gives." Knowledge is seen as a tool which can guide the young career official in the analysis of policy choices/issues.

The Dilemma of the Policy Analyst

When these policy analysts obtain their first jobs, they are likely to face several dilemmas and choices:

(1) Should they be loyal to the organizational interests strongly articulated by those who trained in a different point in history with a different educational program, or should they be loyal to the values of the "true analysts"?

(2) Should they be suspicious of the external information resources, just because such suspicion is regarded as traditional behavior which is in the "best interest" of the organization?

(3) Should they be as unwilling to share information across organizational boundaries as are their superiors and experienced colleagues? Or should the tools of analysis guide their professional behavior?

The data presented in this chapter will suggest that modern policy analysts resolve these dilemmas in a creative manner: Their formal behavior reflects the traditional values of the bureaucracy, which emphasizes the dominance of organizational interests. Informally, however, analysts are guided by values acquired as part of their professional training program; externally generated research is used and information is shared across organizational boundaries.

While investigating the role of knowledge and expertise within a particular policy area, it became clear that both the traditional and the modern values were being maximized concurrently. An informal network of high-level, well-trained young analysts were exchanging information with each other and the top research scholars in the country, while giving the appearance (at the formal level) of adhering to traditional practices. In reading the memorandum written by these analaysts, one would not conclude that external information is being relied on; this conclusion is substantiated in terms of interviews with high-ranking officials.

Evaluation Research in Context

Evaluation research or program evaluation is especially interesting because it raises the classic dilemma of the policy analyst in a somewhat different fashion: Individuals have implicit models for assessment that they have learned over time. Analysts are constantly (that is, on a day-to-day basis) in the position of accepting or rejecting ideas and/or strategies for change that are proposed to them. These "models" are often implicit; yet, they are critical because they serve as the basis for decision-making.

Evaluation research was formally introduced to experienced policy makers (experts) who were being asked to replace their "well-learned" assessment or evaluation models with a new mode of inquiry. This formal model of inquiry was steeped in scientific tradition and legitimated by well-known and respected practitioners—a new tool for the policy analyst. Policy makers were uncomfortable with this new tool of research—it was not as reliable (or perhaps not even as valid) as intuition or experience.

Despite these reservations, program evaluation (or evaluation research) has matured into a discipline with specific training programs. Evaluation as a discipline has received recognition by the U.S. government, particularly the legislative and executive branches, and has been legitimated through legislatively mandated requirements and special offices of departments (for example, the Assistant Secretary for Policy, Planning, and Evaluation), as well as divisions of the Office of Management and Budget and the General Accounting Office.

Evaluation is thought of as a formal component of the problem-solving/policy-making process by academicians and practitioners alike. In academic circles, there is a concern for training professional evaluators or, at a minimum, professionals who understand evaluation and can assess the quality and viability of its findings. These professionals are hired in government agencies, large research institutions, and in the expanding number of for-profit consulting firms.

Evaluation has grown and gained legitimacy more rapidly than most traditional disciplines. In strict economic terms, the demand for evaluation continues to exceed the supply of available, well-trained professionals who are capable of meeting the needs of managers in and out of government.

Evaluation research is a form of social science information that policy makers believe can help them in their problem-solving activities. A 1977 General Accounting Office (GAO) review of the use of social research by national policy makers disclosed high expectations for the utility of information derived from formal evaluation research. More than 70 percent of the respondents, consisting of top management officials in federal agencies, thought that social science should have a substantial or very large effect on the formulation of national policy. In terms of pace, the GAO study showed that 45 percent of the policy makers indicated they were not satisfied with the translation of research results into usable products or into techniques for problem-solving.

There have been a number of explanations put forward to account for the gap between the articulated need for evaluation and the behavior of officials who do not use (or who underutilize) such information.

A CASE OF ACTUAL USE OR OF TRANSLATING RESEARCH INTO ACTION

Given these issues in producing, disseminating, and using evaluation research one can ask the question: How has evaluation research been used; what are some of the major factors which affect utilization? To address these questions, it would be useful to examine how different types of evaluation research are used by policy makers at the national level in the United States.

Unemployment Insurance

The first empirical study reported was limited in scope to the examination of one policy area; this was done to gain an in-depth understanding of the process and quality of research utilization. The policy area chosen for study was the "duration of benefits" area within the context of unemployment insurance policy. Unemployment insurance is a controversial topic of interest in and without the federal government; it commands constant attention and activity with various labor unions, human rights organizations, and university economists, as well as of several federal agencies and Congress.

The duration of benefits issue allows for the examination of some important problems facing those interested in the use of evaluation research: (1) There are significant bureaucratic rivalries built into policy deliberations on this issue. The Department of Labor has jurisdiction over an issue that HEW believes it should be dealing with. HEW claims that "duration of benefits" questions border on welfare policy; as such, these questions should fall under their jurisdiction. (2) The "duration of benefits" issues should allow for problem-solving that will involve the cooperation and coordination of several federal agencies. It also requires coordination with Congress (behavior which is not consistent with traditional bureaucratic practice). (3) The "duration of benefits" issue allows for problem-solving which involves several different sections of the Department of Labor. Thus, it was possible to examine inter- and intraagency use and sharing of information. (4) In the "duration of benefits" in-house and extramural studies have been commissioned. Thus, the study focused on patterns of use of information produced by the federal government as compared with studies produced externally.

Data Base and Study Design

The study was designed to test whether knowledge acquisition processes and utilization patterns in a modern federal bureaucracy level (knowledge development/expertise) can be characterized by the traditional organizational and/or modern policy analyst models of organizational behavior.

The exploratory research focused on the roles of bureaucrats as experts. The role of the expert can be studied by examining a central component of "expert behavior": knowledge acquisition (through training or keeping abreast of current research), processing, and utilization. As already indicated, one policy area was selected to maximize in-depth understanding of the phenomena under study.

The duration of benefits issue seemed ideal because it represented an issue with a discrete and relatively small number of
federal officials involved in making a significant contribution
to the decision-making in the policy area. "Significant contribution" should be thought of as having direct responsibility
for decision-making and/or devoting 10 percent of one's working
time to problem-solving related to this issue. Twenty-eight
federal officials met these criteria.

Having identified this pool of officials within the U.S. Congress (staff); the Department of Labor; the Department of Health,
Education and Welfare; the Office of Management and Budget;
the Council of Economic Advisors, each of the 28 officials was
interviewed. Individuals were identified at each level of the
decision-making hierarchy. Nevertheless, the officials interviewed were in GS-12 to GS-14 positions—high-level civil
servants with an expertise in the policy area under examination.

These face-to-face, in-depth interviews were conducted with
a formal interview instrument. Within the Department of Labor
persons in charge of various sections of the Employment and
Training Administration were interviewed. In the Unemployment
Insurance section, individuals from the Office of Policy Evaluation and Research and the Office of Field Operations were
interviewed. Those responsible for unemployment insurance
within the office of the Assistant Secretary for Policy Evaluation
and Research (Department of Labor) also were interviewed.
Outside the Department of Labor, the staffs of relevant congressional committees, OMB, and the Council of Economic Advisors
were interviewed. Within the Department of Health, Education
and Welfare, two individuals were interviewed who dealt with
unemployment problems as they related to welfare policy.

With the exception of the Department of Labor, where it was
fairly clear from examining the organizational chart who should
be working on particular problems, individuals were identified
through the "snowballing" technique; names were mentioned
by several people of those who made significant contributions
to policy on the duration of benefits issue. Once names were
mentioned two or three times, those named were contacted on an
informal basis.

The interviews focused on identifying the sources of information used by officials working on the duration of benefits issue, the channels (briefings, telephone conversations, formal research reports) used to communicate information to the officials, the levels of use of information, the extent to which information was shared and/or kept secret by officials working in a common problem area, the extent to which officials within the same department communicate with each other and/or share information, and the extent to which officials from different departments communicate with each other when working on this particular issue.

Although this was a case study of one issue area, it offered the advantage of an in-depth understanding based on interviews with all those who made significant contributions to policy deliberations. It should also be noted that the duration of benefits issue represents a "critical" area within the overall context of unemployment insurance policy: It represents an issue that the Congress is concerned with and one that might receive legislative attention in the future. It is, therefore, a highly political issue whose information-related aspects might be different than more routine issues.

HYPOTHESIS

If the results from this study are to be characterized by the traditional pattern of organizational behavior—that is, maximizing organizational interest—one would expect to document a tendency to resist the acquisition and use of information from sources external to the agency, a reliance on one's own staff information on critical issues, a tendency not to share information with other individuals from other government agencies as well as with one's own agency, and acceptance of a general attitude of suspicion for persons and sources of information external to one's own agency.

On the other hand, if the modern policy analyst model were to be validated, one would expect to find a willingness to share information, a tendency to acquire and use information irrespective of its source, and a general attitude of acceptance of all persons and sources of information which may be relevant to the problem under investigation.[1]

FINDINGS

Knowledge for power versus knowledge for enlightenment. As already pointed out, this is a policy area with a wide variety of agencies, researchers, research institutions, and lobby/pressure groups who are concerned and interested in it. All of the actors are potential information producers; they could contribute to the link between knowledge and policy in the duration of benefits area.

As illustrated in Table 1, respondents as a whole rely more on their own in-house staff than other sources of information. There is very little, if any, reliance placed on information from ohter executive branch federal agencies, information generated by Congress, or information provided by consultants. Research institutions outside the department and research generated through departmentally sponsored research programs (Requests for Proposals—RFPs) are also relied on (but not as much information generated by in-house staff). State agencies, who have a stake in this policy area, are used a great deal by some respondents and not at all by others.

These responses give an initial indication that there is probably very little formal sharing of information among agencies; in addition, there may be little coordination of information-generating and information-utilization activities.

Within this context, it is also worth noting that lower-level line staff pay far more attention to outside research institutions, consultants, and information derived from departmentally sponsored RFPs than do upper-level officials.

Form in which information is received. The data on sources of information provide an understanding of what information is acquired. It is also important to document the form in which it is communicated once received. Table 2 illustrates the patterns of communication within the duration of benefits area.

On the basis of these results, several points are worth highlighting: As with the sources of information, researchers do not play major roles in communicating information critical for policy deliberations. More importantly, perhaps, formal channels of communication clearly are not given the same attention as informal channels. "Informal conversations" and "telephone

Table 1: Extent to Which Respondents Have Relied on
the Following Sources of Information[a]

	None[b] 0	Very Little 1	2	3	4	Greatly 5	No Response
In-House Staff	0	3	1	4	3	16	1
Outside Research Institutions	2	1	4	5	10	6	0
Departmentally Sponsored RFPs	2	4	1	5	10	5	1
State Agencies	7	7	1	3	6	4	0
Other Executive Branch Federal Agencies	7	14	2	1	3	0	1
Congress	16	9	0	0	2	1	0
Consultants	13	13	1	1	0	0	0

Number of Respondents = 28

a. The sources have been arranged in descending order according to the extent to which they are relied on.
b. This response category was not actually called for in the questionnaire, but because so many respondents chose to respond in this way this category has been included.

calls" become the medium of communication at all levels of the decision-making hierarchy.

When formal channels of communication are relied on, full written reports and written summaries of reports prepared by staff are preferred over oral briefing (a formal briefing session) and researchers' summaries.

Uses of information. Respondents were also asked to specify the uses made of the information received in this policy area. Table 3 summarizes the reponses to these questions. The interviews initially asked officials to specify what studies were received. Sixty-two studies were mentioned by the 28 respondents. These studies can be divided into four categories:

(1) studies generated by internal staff—staff within a particular division (52 percent),
(2) studies generated by other government agencies (18 percent),
(3) departmentally sponsored RFPs (27 percent), and

Table 2: The Form of Information Received[1]

	Never[2]	Rarely[3]	Some-times[4]	Fre-quently[5]	No Response
Informal conversation	0	0	0	28	1
Telephone call	0	2	1	21	5
Full written report	2	7	4	16	0
Summary written by staff	3	6	4	10	6
Oral briefing	3	12	6	8	0
Summary written by researcher	3	16	5	4	0

Number of respondents = 29

1. The forms of information have been arranged in descending order according to the extent to which they are received.
2. Included in the "Never" category are responses which were categorically negative, such as "never" or "no."
3. Included in the "Rarely" category are affirmative responses which were qualified by such phrases as "rarely," "once in a whole," "tends not to," "if they exist," "only in X particular instance," "not usually," "not very often," or "not many."
4. Included in the "Sometimes" category are affirmative responses which were qualified by such phrases as "sometimes," "not always," "in certain cases," "if there is one—always," "or yes X, but I *rely* on Y."
5. Included in the "Frequently" category are affirmative responses which were qualified by such phrases as "frequently," "usually," "rely on," "tend to rely on," "always," or "yes."

(4) outside research agencies not sponsored by the department (3 percent).

It is particularly significant that over half of the studies mentioned were generated within the division of the officials being interviewed, and 97 percent of the studies cited were completed under some form of departmental and/or governmental control. Indeed, in the case of in-house studies and departmentally sponsored RFPs, agencies can exercise a maximum amount of control over the research process.

The actual pattern of· utilization seemed to be correlated with the nature of the departmental control over the research. Table 4 illustrates that in the case of the "staff studies" *very substantial* and *concrete* uses were made of internally generated

Table 3: Studies Cited as Being Used/or Received on the
Duration of Benefits Issue

Type of Study				
Staff Studies				
P R O D U C E R	Internal/ Division	32	Mathematical	11
			Upjohn	3
	Other Government Agency	11	Center for Naval Research	3
			Brookings	2
	Total	43	Total	19
			Grand Total	62
	Number of Respondents = 28			

NOTE: Each respondent could cite more than one study that was used.

research studies. In only six cases were the results received not used.

By way of contrast, it is interesting to note that in the case of the departmentally sponsored RFPs, (regarding "Outside Studies") very little substantial use is made of these studies and far higher levels of nonutilization were reported.

The Modern Policy Analyst Reexamined

The preceding discussion of knowledge acquisition and utilization behavior of modern bureaucrats in several federal agencies in the United States would seem to validate the traditional organizational behavior model. Officials are suspicious of sources of information which are generated/produced outside their agency; they limit their use of information to that which is produced in-house and provided by their own staff. Indeed, decision makers are reluctant to collect or contract for information from outside their agency or even from a different division within their own agency. Individual decision makers appear to be more comfortable with traditional channels they are familiar with, and whose value they can assess, than with an agency or

Table 4: Specific Uses for Research Studies Cited by Government Officials

	Type of Study			
	Staff Study		Outside Study	
S	White House decision on	3	Issue papers for the president	1
P	construction of program			
E			General background reading	5
C	Staff consultation/meeting	7	Theoretical/philosophical	
I	Estimates/forecast/economic	5	materials	
F	model			
I	Writing general issue papers	14		
C	Design legislation	2	Reading on specific essay	3
U	Write option papers	7		
S	Budget preparation	2		
E	Background reading	8		
	Not Used	6	Not Used	12
	Number of Respondents = 28			

NOTE: Each respondent could cite more than one type of use.

individual with whom they have had little or no experience, or for whom the decision maker has no basis on which to judge the reliability of the information provided.

However, these data reveal that telephone conversations are particularly important for communications *within* and *across* agencies. The data point to the fact that officials rely on informal channels of communication. When something is put in writing, it takes on an aura of *formality* and *certainty* which decision makers are not comfortable with. If the traditional organizational interest model behavior was operating in "ideal-type fashion," formal means of communication would be critical. Thus, it seems to be important to follow up on this finding.

Each respondent was asked to identify the sources of information they relied on for problem-solving activities. Usually, individuals in government were mentioned as the most important information resource—other "experts." These individuals were in the Department of Labor, as well as the Department of Health, Education and Welfare; the Office of Management and Budget; and the Council of Economic Advisors.

As more people were interviewed, it became apparent that this form of informal interagency communication was not limited to a small group of mavericks who were not comfortable with the traditional model of bureaucratic behavior. Through these interviews it was discovered that each of the twenty-eight respondents were "plugged in" to this network through communication with officials within their own department and the other agencies involved with problem-solving on the duration of benefits issue.

The individuals involved in this "network" were identified through the "snow-balling" method; several people were mentioned as being critical, while the same people were mentioned in other interviews and other names were added to the list. Individuals were not considered to be part of the network unless they were mentioned at least three different times.

The network might be represented by the diagram in Figure 1. There are about ten people at the "center" of this network. They are in communication with each other on a regular basis, and at least one of the persons at the "center" has contact with other network members. Through these one-to-one contacts, the "center" is kept informed about the ideas and problem-solving activities of the rest of the members. Through the activities of the persons at the center, each member of the network benefits from the knowledge and information resource of the network as a whole. However, only a small number of network members come in contact with all other members. Each member is in contact with at least five or six other members (on average); as part of these interactions these individuals are sharing information, including the information available to them through informal interaction of other members of the network.

There appears to be a loose network of officials who work in a coordinated fashion. This coordination is not limited to intraagency communication. However, the results of these informal communications are not directly referred to in formal agency memos, meetings, or briefings. Indeed, as one agency official reported: "My boss has instructed me not to refer to communications of other departments. Memos are to reflect my own conclusions and expertise." Thus, several memos may be written on the same subject based on the similar pool of information from different agency perspectives.

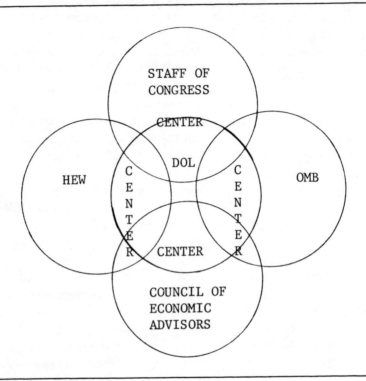

Figure 1: Informal Network

Sources of Information

The data from this study also reveal that the members of this informal network do not rely on in-house studies/research alone. In other words, the same information resources are not being constantly recirculated through a series of informal telephone contacts.

As already reported, the officials interviewed seemed to rely heavily on in-house-generated research on the duration of benefits issue. The same respondents were also asked to identify other kinds of informal or formal information which is used in problem-solving activities on the duration of benefits issue. Table 5 summarizes the responses to this question.

It is evident that these officials rely on a wide variety of information resources, including inputs from interest groups, uni-

Table 5: Other Kinds of Informal or Formal Information Utilized

Newspapers	8	Federal Advisory Council	1
Conferences	3	Congress	1
Journals	2	State Agency	3
In-house Staff Consultation	9	Other Government Agencies	2
University Colleagues	5	Interest Groups	6
		No Other Sources	10

Number of Respondents = 28

NOTE: Each respondent could mention more than one source.

versity colleagues, newspapers, conferences, and journals. Consultation (in-house) with colleagues is also cited as being very important.

Despite the fact that on an informal basis government officials consult a wide variety of diverse information sources, one can legitimately ask: Are these officials keeping abreast of the most up-to-date scholarly research in the area? If these officials can be characterized by the modern policy analyst model, they should not only be sharing information with each other, but should also be familiar with the most up-to-date research.

In consultation with several labor economists at the Princeton University Industrial Relations Center, we were able to identify the most recent scholarly pieces of research in the area: Eight studies were cited as being important from a policy perspective as well as "a contribution to the research literature."

Respondents were asked if they were familiar with the studies and whether or not they used them. Table 6 summarizes the responses to this question.

From an examination of these data, it is evident that in the vast majority of cases respondents were familiar with these studies and had already, at the time of the interview, applied them as part of the problem-solving process. The data undoubtedly point to the existence of a very well-informed network of officials: they are familiar with the most up-to-date research in the policy area they are responsible for. Information is shared across agency lines; officials are aware and make use of a wide variety of knowledge and resources. The training received by these policy analysts is reflected in their communication and research patterns at an informal level.

Table 6: Knowledge of State of the Art Studies

	Never Heard of	Heard of, Not Read	Read, Used Background	Read, Used Substantially
Study No. 1	12	3	13	
Study No. 2		12	16	
Study No. 3	3	6	13	6
Study No. 4		6	7	15
Study No. 5	6	9	10	3
Study No. 6	12	3	7	6
Study No. 7			22	6
Study No. 8			28	

Number of Respondents = 28

Further collaboration of the validity of the modern policy analyst model is found in the response to the question: What are the most important factors in explaining whether or not you use the policy-related information in your work? Five factors were cited as most important: (1) the information is objective and unbiased, (2) the information is timely, (3) the information deals with an important issue, (4) the information has pragmatic implications, and (5) the information is of high technical quality and the methodology is reliable. The least important factors deal with what is identified in the literature as "politicization" of knowledge utilization: "it doesn't raise controversial issues," "it supports previous policy," "it doesn't challenge existing institutional arrangements," "the information does not contribute to inter-agency tensions." Carol Weiss (1978), in a national study on mental health policy-making, also found that these factors were unimportant in expanding the utilization.

These modern experts/policy analysts seem to be concerned with applying knowledge so as to guide the substantive development of the policy-naming process.

Discussion

The findings from this study point to the distinct and important difference between formal and informal systems of communication. Formally, organizations request, process, and imply information resources. As Caplan and Rich (1976) have pointed out, formal systems of communication can be best characterized as reflecting a closed system of decision-making—in the main, the model of maximizing organizational interest. Formally, agencies appeared to follow a set of utilization practice procedures which (a) guarantee the rejection of externally produced information inputs and (b) place an inordinate reliance on agency control and ownership in judging the applicability of policy-related information. In this study, it was possible to verify the existence of a closed decision-making system in the duration of benefits area at the formal level. When asked directly, in an open-ended fashion, about the information resources that are used, the vast majority of respondents stated that in-house research studies were critical because they provided officials with needed information *through regular channels.*

However, at the level of informal briefings and telephone conversations, there appears to be a more open system of communication in decision-making. One official stated: "The channels of information flow here very informally; everyone just talks to everyone else." The existence of this network was only apparent after careful probing on the significance of informal information. Formal channels of communication reflect bureaucratic protection of boundaries, and the informal communications point to a good deal of sharing; this is consistent with the preferred form of communication (informal).

The significance of the empirical results of this study are theoretical; the results provide concepts from which it is possible to organize and give meaning and understanding to knowledge development in policy deliberation.

The case study is limited to an in-depth understanding of highly politicized policy-making areas involving several different federal agencies. However, as decision-making becomes more complex, there are few issue areas that are handled exclusively by one agency—much less than by one branch of the federal government. The results may, therefore, be generalizable to other policy-making areas of the same or similar characteristics.

The Alternative Models

Theoretically, the study points to a need to reexamine what is meant by "the role of the expert" and the application of expertise in modern bureaucratic organizations. To the extent that expertise is equated with knowledge development—including one's technical training and ability to assess up-to-date information—it is evident that both models are operating.

The fact that both are in operation seems to reflect the nature of the reward and incentive system within the executive branch of the federal government. Public officials have always been rewarded for loyalty to their organization and for protecting the interests of that organization. As long as a monopoly over control of information is equated with the central interest of an organization, sharing of information will be resisted.

Indeed, in previous studies of dissemination and uses of information at the federal level, Rich (1977, 1979b) found that information was only disseminated across agency lines at the highest levels of the decision-making hierarchy, and sharing of this kind occurred only rarely. These findings were based on investigation of formal mechanisms for knowledge transfer and utilization. Memos and other documentation were examined as the basis for the conclusions.

There is a logic to these findings from several different perspectives. Bureaucrats are not rewarded for sharing, as this study reveals; they do not formally document it when it occurs. Formal documentation which is open to review and evaluation naturally will reflect the realities of the operating incentive system.

On the other hand, modern bureaucrats were also loyal to the values that their training tells them should be adhered to by an analyst. They seek the best information available—even if this is not apparent from the formal documentation. The informal channels of communication and the network (informal college) which it represents ensures a wide coverage of available information resources. It also provides for a network of experts who are aware of the actions and operations of several agencies working on similar policy problems.

In a broader context, the results of this study forced us to confront the apparent contradiction between the picture of the policy-making process presented to the public and the informal operating procedures followed by middle-level bureaucrats. This contradiction is related to the reward system within government.

The overall conclusion of this analysis is that far more information is shared than we are currently aware of and/or is currently documented. Consequently, experts are put in the position of having to juggle the formal decision-making process with the values that govern their informal behavior. If this type of sharing is to be reflected in formal organizational procedures, then attention needs to be given to the operating reward system.

CONCLUSION

When and if we move closer to D. T. Campbell's notion of an experimenting society (Campbell, 1971a), the professional evaluator will take on an increasingly important role, basically because evaluation will be a critical instrument for planning and social control.

Even if we never realize the "dream" of an experimenting society, it is clear that evaluation activities are a vital part of the policy-making process at all levels of government and in the private sector as well. Further expansion should not continue without a careful assessment of where evaluation is as a field, where it wants to go, and how it might arrive at its objectives in a manner which adheres to agreement on professional standards. In other words, evaluators need to evaluate themselves.

NOTE

1. Both of these descriptions are specified as "ideal types" so as to illustrate the types of behavior which best illustrate both models of bureaucratic behavior: a specified concrete form of behavior as well as attitudes.

REFERENCES

ARROW, K. J. (1974) The Limits of Organization. New York: W. W. Norton.
CAMPBELL, D. T. (1971a) "Methods for the experimenting society." Presented before the Eastern Psychological Association, April 17.
——— (1971b) "Administrative experiments, insitutional records, and non-reactive measures." In W. Evans (ed.) Organizational Experiments. New York: Harper & Row.
——— (1969) "Reforms as experiments." American Psychologist 24: 409-428.
CAPLAN, N. (1976) "The use of program evaluation by federal policy makers at the national level." Presentation at an NIMH-sponsored meeting of the Network of Consultants on Knowledge Transfer, New Orleans.

—— and R. RICH (1976) "Open and closed knowledge inquiry systems: The process and consequences of bureacratization of information policy at the national level." Presented at the OECD Conference on Dissemination of Economic and Social Development Research Results, Bogota, Colombia, June.

CAPLAN, N. et al. (1975) The Use of Social Science Knowledge in Policy Decisions at the National Level. Ann Arbor: Institute for Social Research, University of Michigan.

COOK, T. (1978) "The abuse, misuses and premature utilization of information." Presentation at a conference on "Research Utilization," University of Pittsburgh, School of Graduate Business, September 20-22.

EISENSTADT, S. N. (1969) The Political Systems of Empire. New York: Free Press.

GORDON, A. and D. T. CAMPBELL (1970) "Recommended accountability guidelines for the evaluation of improvements in the delivery of state social services." (unpublished)

GORDON, A. et al. (1975) "Public access to information." Northwestern Law Review 68: 285-286.

GUTTENTAG, M. (1978) Testimony before the Senate Committee on Human Resources, quoted in Evaluation and Change, Special Issue, p. 18.

HAUSER, P. M. (1972) "Statistics and politics." Prepared for the Annual Meetings of the American Statistical Association, August 15.

ILLCHMAN, W. and T. UPHOFF (1971) The Political Economy of Change. Berkeley: University of California Press.

KITUSE, J. and A. V. CICOUREL (1969) "A note on the use of official statistics." Social Problems 11: 131-139.

LEVINE, R. A. (1972) Public Planning: Failure and Redirection. New York: Basic Books.

MORSS, E. and R. F. RICH (1979) Government Information Management. Boulder, CO: Westview Press.

NAY, J. et al. (1978) Testimony before the Senate Committee on Human Resources, quoted in Evaluation and Change, Special Issue, pp. 12-13.

RICH, R. F. (1979a) "Editor's Introduction," American Behavioral Scientist. January/February.

—— (1979b) The Use of Social Science Information and Public Policy Making. San Francisco: Jossey-Bass.

—— (1977) "The use of social science informatioin by federal bureaucrats: knowledge for action versus knowledge for understanding." In C. Weiss (ed.) The Uses of Social Research in Public Policy Making. Lexington, MA: D. C. Heath.

SCHLESINGER, A. M., Jr. (1973) The Imperial Presidency. Boston: Houghton-Mifflin.

SIBLEY, J. (1972) "Students say a policeman tried to falsify a report of a holdup." New York Times, November 23: 5, 40.

SKOLNICK, J. H. (1975) Justice Without Trial. New York: John Wiley.

WEISS, C. H. (1978) "The use of evaluation research." Presented at a conference on "Research Utilization," University of Pittsburgh, School of Business, September 20-22.

WILLIAMS, W. (1975) Social Policy Research and Analysis. New York: Elsevier.

VON HENTIG, H. (1974) The Criminal and His Victim. New Haven, CT: Yale University Press.

—— (1941) "Remarks on interaction of perpetrator and victim." Journal of Criminal Law and Criminology 31.

PART III

Evaluation and Policy:

Nonfederal Experiences

Jonas Waizer

New Jersey Department of Human Services

6

EVALUATION FOR THE DEVELOPMENT OF STATE POLICY IN COMMUNITY MENTAL HEALTH
Is There Life After Birth for Policy-Oriented Evaluations?

Frequently analyses of the impact of policy-oriented evaluation on the process of governmental decision-making suffer from a narrow perspective of what constitutes effective utilization. In a review of federal evaluation studies, Michael Patton (1978) found that such research is utilized more often than is generally credited, but not in the timely fashion nor with the direct applicability that is generally considered essential for "successful" program evaluation.

Patton extracted from the files of the Department of Health, Education and Welfare a sample of federal health program evaluations which met his research criteria. He conducted follow-up studies and identified two factors which appeared to influence effective utilization: (1) studies in which evaluators had taken personal interest in reinforcing the acceptance of their data and (2) political situations in which critical decision makers or information-users had originally focused the goals of the research study rather than simply approving the projects. Patton concluded that the criteria for studying utilization of policy-oriented evaluation must be broadened to reflect the identification of the relevant decision makers and of the political process through which information is incorporated. He indicated that utilization is gradual rather than immediate, and that the timeliness of the feedback is secondary to its relevance for political decision makers.

The recent history of New Jersey's mental health policy reform substantiates Patton's findings. In this case influential decision makers had been active in designing the specifications of a study commissioned to assess the need for institutional and community mental health services. The study, described in detail below, indicated a need for reallocation of support to community mental health. By the common standard of data utilization, the evaluation might have been judged unsuccessful. This was indicated by the fact that the needs assessment data never played a substantive role in subsequent funding decisions. However, the actual criterion selected for judging research utilization in this case was the increased state government funding for community mental health over time. By this measurement, the impact of the needs assessment proved substantial. As Patton recommends, recognition of a broader criterion which credits the political process and the roles of the influential decision makers appears to offer a more valid basis for determining the impact of policy-oriented evaluation.

Patton also appeared justified in recommending patience in determining the influence of utilization-focused evaluation. As was the case in New Jersey, administrative interest in evaluation research diminished as the additional funding became available for the new community mental health programs, and the policy-oriented evaluation appeared to have outlived its usefulness. The attenuated interest in data utilization, however, was temporary. By remaining attuned to the shifting information needs of the influential administrative decision makers, program evaluation adopted a new role with increased activity and significance within the mental health system. The incorporation of evaluation in policy development seems to go through a gradual transformation directed by the political process.

Windle and Neigher (1978) have indicated that there are a number of evaluation models which, in their view, are potentially conflicting. In New Jersey's case, it appears that the advocacy role for evaluation research diminished following the needs assessment.

At the same time, an increased demand for *accountability* developed. As the new community mental health policies actually became implemented, the resulting programs began to encounter serious political resistance. In reaction to growing criticism, the key policy makers considered it important to test and study those programs which grew out of the recent changes. The rapid shift in evaluation design focusing on the development of accountability-oriented research to accommodate the important information users, after having originally developed an advocacy-oriented data base, proved to be the key to the continued impact of evaluation research in ongoing policy development.

It may be of value to investigate specifics of the interplay between the program evaluation efforts and New Jersey's emerging community mental health policy reform, in order to consider the factors which contributed to the cycle of utilization-focused evaluation research. The changes in New Jersey's mental health system during the past four years can be considered a reflection of the emergence of a national policy toward community mental health.

In 1974 the Department of Health and the Department of Human Services were instructed by Governor Byrne to jointly develop a comprehensive mental health plan in compliance with federal law (P.L. 94-631). As a result, the New Jersey Mental Health Planning Committee was convened. In 1975 the committee commissioned a needs assessment study of the clientele treated in public psychiatric hospitals and community agencies, including community mental health centers (CMHCs). A research team used a global level of functioning instrument (Carter and Newman, 1976) to assess patients on a continuous scale of nine increasing levels of functioning behavior. Over 5000 community clients and 3000 of the 9600 institutionalized patients were surveyed. Partial results are shown in Table 1 (A Manual for Reform, 1976).

Treatment histories and demographics of the clients were also collected and analyzed. The major findings of New Jersey's report (1976) were subsequently confirmed at the national level in studies by the Government Accounting Office (1977) and the

Table 1: Comparison of Distribution of Levels of Functioning Between Community Agency Sample and Hospital Sample

Level of Functioning	Community Agency		State and County Hospitals	
	No.	%	No.	%
Low				
I	49	1.0	606	21.7
II	105	2.1	874	31.3
III	161	3.1	409	14.6
IV	292	5.8	339	12.1
V	789	15.5	217	7.8
VI	950	18.7	96	3.4
VII	1,699	33.5	158	5.7
VIII	816	16.1	84	3.0
IX	214	4.2	10	0.4
High				

	Community Agencies		State and County Hospitals	
	No.	%	No.	%
I-III	315	6.2	1,889	67.6
IV-VI	2,031	40.0	652	23.3
VII-IX	2,729	53.8	252	9.1

President's Commission on Mental Health (1978). Essentially, the study indicated that (1) patients discharged from state psychiatric hospitals were more likely to return to those state hospitals if and when they were in need of any mental health services; (2) between one-third and two-thirds of the institutionalized population could be immediately and adequately served in less restrictive community settings according to their level of functioning scores; and (3) that CMHCs and other community mental health agencies had failed to adequately serve those individuals discharged from state hospitals. The New Jersey study concluded:

Our survey confirms the fact that the two systems [institutional and community] are serving largely separate clienteles. If we are to construct a truly community based system of care for all patients, the two must be integrated [A Manual for Reform, 1976: 17].

Based on the finding of this survey, the Division of Mental Health and Hospitals underwent a major reorganization. A new policy of community mental health was introduced, predicated on the philosophy of "normalization" expounded by Wolf Wolfensberger (1972) and governed by the principles of "unified services" and "care in the least restrictive alternative."

One additional policy was introduced to radically alter the nature of New Jersey's community mental health system. Priority was to be given to the development of Community Support Services for the deinstitutionalized patient, rather than to the expansion of traditional mental health outpatient or aftercare services. The concept of community mental health had been aggressively expanded; it was to emphasize the need for funding social, residential, vocational, and recreational services to supplement traditional therapeutic and rehabilitational services in order to develop a comprehensive human services model specifically for deinstitutionalized patients. As subsequently reflected by NIMH policy, the basis of this community mental health policy was the assumption that deinstitutionalized or mentally ill patients were stigmatized and had been deprived of services that were available to other handicapped or indigent populations. The state adopted an advocacy position for mental health clients with other human services agencies or provided for the direct funding of nonmental health support services by the mental health care system. The de-institutionalized patient was to be assisted in adjusting to community living to avert a cycle of rejection and expulsion through repeated institutionalization.

The division proceeded to implement these new community mental health policies. Since 1975, New Jersey's state and county hospitals and grant-in-aid outpatient programs have been reorganized to provide a single system of mental health services. Deinstitutionalized patients are expected to be given priority service in all state-subsidized programs and, through voluntary agreements, at the CMHCs. Through affiliation agreements and centrally coordinated negotiations with the CMHCs in the state, new emphasis has been placed on producing a unified services model. In addition, a county-contained system of mental health planning has been developed to coordinate state, county, CMHCs, and other community mental health services in each locale.

The state legislature supported the division's implementation of the Community Support Program (CSP). Following the needs assessment study, funds were diverted from the state institutional budgets and, along with Title XX funds, special contracts were awarded to local service agencies. The contracts specified that agencies primarily serve patients emerging from public psychiatric hospitals and provide community adjustment services— including supervised and unsupervised housing, social and legal advocacy, vocational training, screening and referral, home-making, transportation, community-based alcoholism services, and programs from pretrial detainers. These supplement the traditional therapeutic outpatient and aftercare services provided through state grant-in-aid programs and CMHCs.

The planners of New Jersey's reform originally expected the contract services to directly reduce the state hospital populations. They had two distinct objectives for contracts: (1) to serve chronic patients during the transition phase from psychiatric hospitalization to community residence, using supervised contract placements and the development of social supports in the community, and (2) to divert inappropriate admissions to the state hospitals by also accepting individuals who could benefit from treatment in the less restrictive settings.

The first three CSP contracts negotiated in 1975 grew to the current level of 55, totaling $8 million, with over 5,000 clients served annually. The successful impact of the original need assessment study in attracting funds and support was undoubtedly influenced by the unique position of the research's sponsors as the administrative heads of the state's health and human services systems.

Evaluation research, however, was not active in the development of the actual contracting system beyond the original assessment study, which advocated additional funding. While the successful impact of evaluation was demonstrated, the continued survival of evaluation research was, at best, uncertain from the perspective of the key policy makers. Within the political process, evaluation research no longer had a critical role, although its theoretical value in decision-making was widely acknowledged.

At this time, an opportunity arose for the shift in the role of evaluation. In the complex interplay among governmental policy development, program funding, and evaluation the original designers of the CSP found themselves in the position of having to defend their achievements to the state legislature. As a result, program evaluation was invoked to respond to the new information demands.

In 1977 a crisis budget situation in the state resulted in a careful reassessment of all human services funding. The mental health CSP program was reviewed by legislative analysts, who criticized it for failing to serve the priority population and for lacking an accountability system. Specifically, the analysts claimed that they felt the contracts had overextended service to less disordered mental health clients, who were being admitted directly from the community on the justification that they had been "diverted" from unnecessary public psychiatric hospitalizations. The analysts also questioned the "chronicity" of those state hospital patients who were accepted into the program, suggesting that short-term, acute patients were more rapidly accepted by the contract programs. They argued that the CSP initiative should be curtailed until these issues were addressed. Ironically, these are the same criticisms which had been leveled at the federal CMHC program.

In contrast, the division sought expanded support for its community mental health policy. The contract program had originally emphasized taking those people directly out of state psychiatric hospitals who could exist in the community if provided with needed living supports and appropriate service linkages. In the last several years, however, it had become increasingly clear that thousands of previously hospitalized clients living in the community as a result of depopulation efforts in the 1960s and early 1970s also needed support services to prevent future hospital readmissions. The population in need had been underestimated. The CSP project continued to be jeopardized through the early part of 1978. In retrospect, the source of the conflict revolved around a lack of agreement or understanding of the nature of the population to be served by the CSP project.

Just before this budget crisis in 1977, the division was awarded a National Institute of Mental Health (NIMH)-CSP State's Strategy Development Grant. The purpose was to develop a strategy for negotiating CSP services for mental health clients from other established human services organizations and to expand on the unified services model. The federal grant provided resources to conduct additional needs assessment for this target population and to document the progress of different CSP strategies.

In coordination with an NIMH evaluation task force, New Jersey had developed clearer criteria for the study of this target population. The following operational definition was developed to identify the deinstitutionalized patient:

In accordance with Division of Mental Health and Hospital's policy, contract clients must meet the Community Support Program's target population eligibility requirements.

In order to be eligible for contract services, within the CSP target population criteria, a potential client must meet *all* the following four conditions, inclusively:

1. 18 years or older.

2. Diagnosis: Mentally disabled adults whose primary disability is emotional exluding patients whose primary diagnosis is developmental disability, retardation, organic brain syndrome, or chronic substance abuse. Criteria: APA DSM-II diagnostic codes for psychoses not attributed to physical conditions (295-298), neuroses (300), and personality disorder (301).

3. Level of Function/Care: Individuals are program eligible if they presently require substantial assistance in the areas of personal self-maintenance, social functioning skills, vocational/educational guidance and community living skills. Individuals are not program eligible if they require continuous care

or supervision as the result of their inability to handle personal self-maintenance situations, therefore requiring continuous nursing care, or if they pose an imminent physical treat to themselves or to others.

4. At the time of initiation, this client must satisfy one or more of these histories of psychiatric hospitalization:

   a. Currently resides in a psychiatric hospital for at least six months of continued stay.

   b. Currently resides in a psychiatric hospital with a history of hospitalization cumulatively adding to at least six months.

   c. Currently resides in a psychiatric hospital with a history of two or more admissions within a 12 month period.

   d. Currently resides in the community but has a history of past psychiatric hospitalizations cumulatively adding to at least six months throughout his or her lifetime.

   e. Currently resides in the community but has a history of at least three admissions to psychiatric hospitals within the last two years of the date of admission to this program.

This definition itemizes the characteristics of the chronic psychiatric patient by specifying age, diagnosis, history of psychiatric hospitalization, and includes a measure of level of functioning (Carter and Newman, 1976). The concept of a target population of deinstitutionalized patients was not novel; it had been part of the intent of the original program in 1975 and was the basic tool in the original needs assessment. The operational definition, however, was a refinement based on subsequent work in the division and NIMH.

The definition of CSP clients was used during 1978 in a series of county-specific studies to determine the size and characteristics of the target population serviced by public psychiatric hospitals, community contract and grant agencies, CMHCs, and, where possible, by other human services agencies. The objective was to provide a comprehensive data base for planning unified services to the target population of deinstitutionalized patients.

Seeking a mechanism to improve the accountability of the CSP contract system more rapidly, the key decision makers (the division's administration) reviewed the operational definition of the target population. The inclusion of level of functioning as part of the definition was carefully considered. It was noted that the measure could provide data for interagency planning and auditing contract compliance to program objectives, as well as for generating outcome studies. Finally, it was agreed that the definition was sufficiently broad to include the large population of historically "deinstitutionalized" patients "dumped" into the community over the last 20 years, as well as those still in the hospitals. The decision to incorporate and emphasize a formal, operationally defined target population as representing the CSP policy was made in mid-1978. The Office of Program Evaluation was expanded to monitor services provided by contracts to the target population and to examine the outcome of services using the level of functioning scale. This is now being conducted through a monthly reporting system.

A survey of the CSP contracts was conducted by the office and 68 percent of the clients were found to satisfy the target population definition. Since then, the community mental health policy has been tightened to limit services to this target population under the CSP contracts.

In developing its accountability system for the contracts, the division addressed the major concern of the legislative analysts that the service programs were subject to abuse. The information system monitors the compliance of the clientele to the target population definition and the program outcome through the level of functioning measurement. The legislative analysts expressed satisfaction with the mechanisms as meeting the need for improved program accountability and focus of clientele, and their resistance has been attenuated, at least temporarily. The introduction of an accountability model for evaluation was effective in reducing growing resistance to the emerging community mental health policy. This outcome easily might have been overlooked as evidence of the effective utilization and impact of evaluation on policy development.

A final indication of the impact of the program evaluation effort is that, as a result of this experience, policy makers are reviewing other mental health funding systems for the purpose of developing operationally defined target populations and for conducting future needs assessment and process evaluation studies. Task forces are currently reviewing specifications for emotionally disturbed children. We anticipate an expanded and more effective role for program evaluation through increased utilization of research as data concerning target populations become the focus of mental health planning and program development in New Jersey.

The original need for advocacy evaluation appeared inversely related to funding level. As legislative support for program development grew, attention to evaluation data diminished. Program implementation, however, appeared to attract resistance and required a different type of information. Evaluation of a different nature was then indicated.

In New Jersey's case, Patton's finding has been substantiated. The close partnership of program evaluation staff with the key decision makers could be considered to have influenced the successful utilization of the research, but only through the adoption of broad criteria which accepts increased program funding and decreased political resistance, rather than direct measures of data utilization.

A SHIFT IN ORIENTATION

The shift in evaluation from advocacy to accountability, while serendipitous rather than planned, may seem entirely political. The question remains whether the actual research data ever will be utilized and have any impact on policy development, or whether they will always remain incidental to the political process.

The division's commitment to adopting an operational definition for its priority target population has created a situation in which continued and even more extensive broad-scale evaluation research is both possible and desirable. For example, combined with the use of budget information, level of functioning measures in the CSP contracts will permit a series of cost-benefit studies. Participation by decision makers in designing the evaluation methodology in the expectation that it will serve their needs for ongoing budgetary support should enhance the utilization of specific reseach findings, and their commitment to the actual data will increase as they continue to rely on it for budgetary defense.

With the growth of these accountability systems within the division, there are indications of changes in the characteristics of the population served by the contracts toward those of the target populations. As more specific data become available, program managers—as well as policy makers—will be compelled to seriously consider their impact. The creation of influential evaluation research in policy development seems linked to the information needs and decision-making processes of the key policy makers. As always, however, these efforts must be conducted with full cognizance of the political realities of policy setting and program development.

REFERENCES

A Manual for Reform of New Jersey's Mental Health Care System, Final Report of the New Jersey Mental Health Planning Committee (1976) Available from New Jersey Division of Mental Health and Hospitals, Trenton, New Jersey.

CARTER, D. E. and F. L. NEWMAN (1976) A Client-Oriented System of Mental Health Service Delivery and Program Management: A Workbook and Guide (DHEW Publications No. (ADM) 76-307). Washington, DC: U.S. Government Printing Office.

PATTON, M. O. (1978) Utilization-Focused Evaluation. Beverly Hills, CA: Sage.

Report to the Congress by the Comptroller General of the United States: Returning the Mentally Disabled to the Community: Government Needs to do More. (1977) Government Accounting Office (HRD-76-152).

Task Panel Reports Submitted to the President's Commission on Mental Health. (1978) Available from the Superintendent of Documents. Washington, DC: U.S. Government Printing Office.

WINDLE, C. and W. NEIGHER (1978) "Ethical problems in program evaluation: advice for trapped evaluators." Evaluation and Program Planning 1 (2): 97-107.

WOLFENSBERGER, W. et al. (1972) The Principle of Normalization in Human Services. Toronto, Canada: National Institute of Mental Retardation through Leonard Crainford.

William D. Neigher
Saint Clare's Hospital CMHC

7

EFFORT AND INFLUENCE
Enhancing the Impact of Mental Health Program Evaluation at the Agency Level

This chapter deals with the impact of program evaluation on policy in a health services setting. Specifically, it addresses evaluation and its utility in the federal Community Mental Health Centers (CMHC) program. Perhaps most importantly, its perspective is from the local agency evaluator, usually one or two people out of about one hundred CMHC staff who look at program effectiveness. Sometimes their function is shared with clinical or administrative responsibilities; others devote their full time to it. While the CMHC program began in 1963 (Bloom, 1977), formal program evaluation requirements did not materialize until the CMHC amendments of 1975 (PL 94-63). Centers are currently required to spend two percent of their operating cost on evaluation—potentially more than $18 million using the latest NIMH figures (NIMH, 1978).

What are the taxpayers buying for the dollars? Is it money well spent? Does it have a substantial and lasting impact on the policies of these agencies? These are good questions. We would assume that program evaluation would not be mandated if its track record did not merit it. The record, however, underscored by commissions and study committees (Patton, 1978), supports the view that "evaluation results have not exerted significant influence on program decisions." On the other hand, the record of

---

AUTHOR'S NOTE: *Susan Neigher and John Kalafat made helpful comments on an ealier draft of this chapter. This is an expanded version of a paper presented at the Third Annual Meeting of the Evaluation Research Society, Washington, D.C., 1978.*

social service programs themselves is less than something to cheer about:

> If there is any empirical law that is emerging from the past decade of widespread evaluation research activities, it is that the expected value for any measured effect of a social program is zero. In short, most programs, when properly evaluated, turn out to be ineffective or at best marginally accomplishing their set aims. There are enough exceptions to prevent this empirical generalization from being phrased as the "Iron Law of Social Program Evaluation," but the tendency is strong enough to warrant placing bets on negative evaluation outcomes in the expectation of making a steady but modest side income [Rossi, 1978:574].

The problems of utilizing program evaluation for planned change are also well known. Attkisson, Brown, and Hargreaves (1978) reprise the familiar litany: problems with validity, issues of relevance and timeliness, differing perceptions of evaluation between evaluators and program managers, and poor organizational responsiveness to evaluation findings.

In spite of this, there is evidence that evaluation research has made a contribution to the mental health care delivery system and that its opportunities for future impact remain promising (Attkisson, and Nguyen, 1978). In fact, much of the remainder of this chapter is about "promises." These promises, like all others, have their share of perils as well for the evaluator in the mental health agency.

Critically examining issues about the impact of evaluation research on policy depends to a large extent on one's perspective —an external evaluator charged with program monitoring and accountability often has views different from the internal, agency evaluator hired to help program management improve their services. Whatever an evaluator's position, however, program evaluators soon discover that there are a number of other evaluation perspectives. In Figure 1 we identify four such evaluation perspectives (Neigher, 1979:10).

Let us consider, for example, a transitional apartment program for former state psychiatric hospital patients returning to the

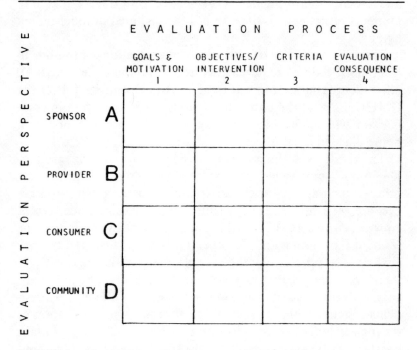

SOURCE: Landsberg, Neigher, Hammer, Windle, and Woy, 1979.

Figure 1: Evaluation Perspectives Matrix

community. In planning an evaluation of the program, it is help-ful to look at the evaluation process from each of the four evalua-tion perspectives: (A) *sponsor* (for example, a State Division of Mental Health), (B) *provider* (a federally funded CMHC under PL 94-63, (C) *the program's consumers* (ex-psychiatric patients) and (D) *community residents* (the residents in the neighborhood surrounding the program).

Obviously, an evaluator cannot always consider each per-spective in depth; often each perspective has its own "evaluator." It is often desirable, however, to look at how each perspective views the program and ultimately at how it will use its "evaluation data" to affect the program. Using the example above, the sponsor (A-1) operates the program to reduce the state hospital population by (A-2) funding agencies through state grants and (A-3) monitoring levels of service "contracts" that link numbers of patients to time frames for sheltered or independent living.

The agency, a CMHC, develops its transitional program to meet both federal requirements and community needs (B-1). After identifying appropriate residences and hiring staff (B-2), the CMHC looks at the cost/effectiveness of this program in comparison with continued state hospital residence and boarding home placement (B-3).

The residents of the program have mixed motivations for participation—some view it as a means of getting out of the hospital; others reluctantly are discharged or adjudicated into the program because their hospitalization is no longer justified under recent court decisions (C-1). By their degree of participation in the residents' program and in other CMHC services (C-2), they evaluate the program by the changes they feel in the quality of their lives—that is, their psychosocial independence C-3. Experience with this type of program residence had led many area residents to actively oppose such efforts through zoning variances or through efforts at community organization (D-1). Their efforts—overt or passive (D-2)—and what they read or hear (or fear) about the program (whether accurate or not) often is the information used to make judgments about the program (D-3).

The consequences of a "good" or "bad" summative evaluation are as varied for each evaluator perspective as are the other aspects. Sponsors can stop funding, the agency may find that both cost and outcome are higher than expected, residents may "drop out," and neighbors may decide to take action against the program. Our point is that by considering these four evaluation perspectives and possible evaluation consequences *up front*, before the evaluation is begun, evaluators can plan their studies based on the pragmatics of decision and consequence.

THE AGENCY-BASED EVALUATOR

Because this article is written from the perspective of an agency-based evaluator, a few words about this particular evaluator are in order. As a traditionally trained experimental social psycholgist, I procreated my field by teaching undergraduates social psychology. I encouraged them to enter social research in the real world, a task in which I regrettably had little experience at the time.

I had read Donald Campbell (1969):

The experimenting society I have in mind would initiate programs and realistically evaluate the outcomes. In the case of failure, going on to new programs and, in the case of success, retaining these as policy, using the best of science to design programs.

Armed with this mantra and frustrated with academic life, I went to New Jersey in 1973 to become one of the state's first program evaluation directors in a CMHC. I was convinced that shortly after my arrival the "experimenting society" was only months away; and after that, could the programs of the Great Society be very far off? The answer was "*Very* far off."

My experience is not unique; many program evaluators without formal training or experiential internship work in a human services environment which is often hostile or insensitive to the evaluation process. Furthermore, there is a great deal of latitude in the extent to which my own evaluation efforts have had a lasting influence upon CMHC policy. Two themes run through these concerns.

The first is that agency evaluators working under multiple funding and accountability requirements usually experience *inconsistent role demands* which often interfere with the evaluation process. The second is that despite a great deal of "hand-wringing" about low utilization of evaluation data, this is more within the evaluators' locus of control than they admit —we can identify evaluation's likely outcomes and program managers' action decisions *much sooner* in the evaluation process than is usually the case in practice.

A basic response to both of these points is best introduced within the context of priorities assigned by CMHC evaluators to their activities.

Table 1: HEW Region II Research and Evaluation Survey in
Community Mental Health Centers (1975 and 1977 data)

Community Mental Health Center Evaluation Activities	Priority Ranking			Stage of Development	
	Pre	Post	Expert[a]	Pre	Post
MIS	1	1	1	1	1.5
Needs assessment	2	5	3	3	3.5
Utilization	3	2	2	2	1.5
Impact	8	7	8.5	11	11
Consumer evaluation	4	4	4.5	4	5
Treatment outcome	5	3	4.5	6.5	3.5
Staff attitude	10	11	11	10	9
Planning	6.5	8	6	6.5	7
Cost effectiveness	6.5	6	8.5	8	10
C&E for community groups	9	9.5	10	5	6
C&E center administration	11	9.5	7	9	8
	N=38	N=25	N=10		
		(22 Matching Pre)			

NOTE: Pretest: 1975; Posttest: 1977.
SOURCE: Landsberg, Hammer, and Neigher, 1978.
a. Recognized authority in mental health program evaluation.

In 1975 the community mental health centers in HEW Region
II (New York, New Jersey, Puerto Rico, and the Virgin Islands)
completed a questionnaire about priorities assigned to their
program evaluation activities. The questionnaire was again
distributed in 1977, identifying changes and priorities that may
have been determined or influenced by the passage of the
program evaluation requirements of the 1975 amendments of the
CMHC legislation (Landsberg et al., 1978). A number of
nationally recognized program evaluation authorities in mental
health were also asked to complete the 1975 questionnaire. Table
1 presents the preliminary data analysis from those two surveys.
While the ordering of the evaluation activities is interesting and
the changes in priorities are noteworthy, our attention focuses on
the evaluation activities aimed at making program evaluation
more comprehensible to community groups and CMHC adminis-

tration. The consistent lack of emphasis placed on these two aspects of program evaluation, both during the pre- and post-questionnaires and by the initial assessment by the panel of experts, underscores a primary reason for the underutilization of program evaluation findings: neglect of those who ultimately must use the information.

The core competencies for successful mental health program evaluation have been described in a number of places (Attkisson et al., 1978b); they constitute skills and methodology, conceptualization and interpersonal qualities. To make mental health program evaluation more identifiable to evaluators in other fields, Table 2 summarizes some of these skills and competencies along the dimensions listed above.

Using some of these activities as a framework, we can illustrate ways of carrying out these activities that can enhance or limit the effect of evaluation on agency policy. The scope of this discussion is necessarily limited, however, and readers looking for a more complete discussion on how to increase the utilization of evaluation research do well to consult more comprehensive sources (Patton, 1978; Davis and Salasin, 1975).

What we are trying to avoid in each evaluation area is best described by Michael Patton in his recent book, *Utilization-Focused Evaluation:* "It's a great study, really well done. We can see you did a lot of work, but it doesn't tell us anything we want to *know*" (1978, p. 72). We might add a new last line: "It doesn't tell us what we wanted to *hear*."

ROLE CLARIFICATION

Who is the local agency evaluator "beholden" to? Funders? Consumers? Administration? From the evaluation perspective matrix in Figure 1, it is apparent that we are "beholden" to *everyone*, each with their own agenda. Are we, as has been suggested, whores who sell out to the highest bidder? B. Bloom (1977) addresses the first of seven principles to CMHC staff:

Principle 1. Regardless of where your paycheck comes from, *think of yourself as working for the community.* Mental-health

Table 2: CMHC Program Evaluation Staff Resources Assessment

Resource	Knowledge[a]	Experience[b]
Methodological:		
1 Program evaluation techniques (outcome/ process evaluation, GAS)	[ ]	[ ]
2 Social and experimental research design (including quasi-experimental approaches)	[ ]	[ ]
3 Information system management (including computer analysis, IMIS, report preparation)	[ ]	[ ]
4 Needs assessment techniques (public health, demography, epidemiology techniques)	[ ]	[ ]
5 Cost accounting (cost-finding/rate-setting procedures, cost-effectiveness models)	[ ]	[ ]
6 Written communication skills (writing technical reports for nontechnical audiences)	[ ]	[ ]
Conceptual:		
1 CMHC theory and legislation (particularly as relates to accountability and administration)	[ ]	[ ]
2 Organizational theory and systems analysis (role of evaluation in decision-making)	[ ]	[ ]
d 3 State government and mental health administration (accountability mechanisms, funding structure)	[ ]	[ ]
d 4 Identification of workable alternatives from analysis of evaluation data	[ ]	[ ]
5 Mental health delivery system	[ ]	[ ]
d 6 Appreciation of clinical treatment perspective in CMHC setting	[ ]	[ ]

Interpersonal; Personality Traits and Skills	Rating[c]
1 Ability to work with interdisciplinary team	[ ]
2 Consultation skills in program evaluation	[ ]
d 3 Listening skills	[ ]
d 4 Personal organizational ability (structure tasks, meet deadlines)	[ ]
d 5 Ability to work with those who perceive evaluation as a threat	[ ]
d 6 Tact	[ ]
d 7 Empathy	[ ]
d 8 Compassion	[ ]

a. 1, No Previous knowledge, to 7, Extensive knowledge.
b. 1, No Previous experience, to 7, Extensive experience in similar setting.
c. 1, Absence of trait or liability, to 7, Strong personal asset.
d. From *Program Evaluation in the State Mental Health Agency*, NIMH, 1976.

programs in the community should be determined by a process of negotiation open to *all members of the community*. The ultimate power for deciding the nature of the community-based mental-health program should rest with the community, and the mental-health professional should work in the community only as long as he or she feels a sense of congruence between the program desired by the community and his or her own personal and professional value systems [Bloom, 1977:260].

Can agency evaluators live with this? A more important question is, can agencies?

We would all acknowledge that there is *no single role* or model for a program evaluator that isomorphically applies to all evaluation contexts. In a recent paper entitled "Ethical Problems In Program Evaluation: Advice For Trapped Evaluators," Chuck Windle and I identified three such models (Windle and Neigher, 1978): An *"amelioration model"* generating better information for our program's own decision-makers; an *accountability model*," focusing on public data disclosure and citizen participation in evaluation; and an *"advocacy model"* in which the evaluation is designed to enhance the program's interests in the competition for resources. While each model inherently has its own set of problems, we argued that ethical problems in program evaluation are increased when conflicting or incompatible evaluation models are applied concurrently.

If managers do not expect program evaluators to be "hung up on the truth" or compulsive about public accountability, then the results of an evaluation study where these factors *suddenly* become issues are likely to be ignored. At the same time, evaluators who structure the evaluation process to include only those decision makers *supportive* of the program or who place their efforts where "*the good results*" are, in a self-serving manner, reduce their creditability and the ultimate utility of this and future evaluation efforts. I will illustrate this point shortly.

INFORMATION MANAGEMENT

For things to happen even in a moderate-sized CMHC requires an increasing amount of information management. The management of a clinical and demographic data base is usually the responsibility of the program evaluation department. An integrated management information system is required for CMHCs under PL 94-63, and specified in the NIMH Research and Evaluation Guideline.

> The capability to collect and integrate data on clients, staff, funds, and services delivered is basic to program evaluation although the routine operation of such information systems is not itself program information [NIMH, 1977].

This section from NIMH's draft Guidelines for Program Evaluation in CMHCs under PL 94-63 emphasizes two important aspects of data collection in relation to program evaluation activities. First, the information gathered must be integrated across several key variables, addressing the familiar evaluation question, "Who does what to whom with what effect?" Simple utilization data as compiled for an annual report to funders (such as the NIMH Biometry Inventory) may serve an accountability function for the agency, but this information alone, detached from the ability to compare units of clinical service (for example, number of sessions) with units of cost (or a measure of clinical effectiveness of treatment), diminishes the potential of an information system to have an impact on the overall quality of care.

The second important distinction outlined in the guidelines is the relationship between management information system (MIS) and domains of program evaluation. Client utilization data, even though aggregated in cohorts meaningful to the program (such as the number of male children under 14 seen by a children outreach unit), become evaluative in nature only when those data are compared with other sources of information, such as agency goals and objectives or normative data (an expected level of client contact for the children's unit) or special client characteristics (long problem duration without prior contact with a mental health agency). At the level of individual clinical record-keeping, the MIS also may play an important role in a CMHC or agency quality assurance program. This MIS may be able to flag clients who experience problems from the service systems (continuity of care), provide source material for retrospective clinical audits or clinical care studies, or identify individuals whose treatment histories suggest the need for quality assurance review (Landsberg et al., 1979).

The process of developing an integrated management information system is a difficult one, tempered by the need to generate data to program managers and to provide accountability data to NIMH's Biometry Branch. The process must be responsive to reporting needs at the local county, state, and federal levels; consider the availability and accessibility of information currently generated by the various CMHC components; and avoid duplication of data collection whenever possible (see Smith and Sorensen, 1974; Chapman, 1976).

Having helped to design and implement MISs at several CMHCs, and having spent more than four years at the state level in developing a statewide Mental Health Information System, I have noted a few realities. Following these few simple principles will practically guarantee *little* or *no* impact from data generated from any MIS:

(1) Sell the *system*. To err is human, but to really mess things up you need a computer. Minicomputers are on the rampage in mental health. Sell your director and board on nuts, bolts, bits, bites, DOS, RPG, and bisynchronous data communication links.

(2) Promise everyone that "the system" will answer all of their questions and meet all of their needs—the system *will* take a while to develop, but by two months from Thursday things ought to be looking up.

(3) Assume program directors will understand the reports, read the printouts, and see the "obvious" historical trends and implications.

(4) Assume that program directors know how to relate the data to program goals, current service functioning, and future decisions.

Keep score, as you watch the inevitability of the following six stages:

(1) Wild enthusiasm, followed by
(2) total disappointment,

(3) total confusion,
(4) the search for the guilty,
(5) the persecution of the innocent and, finally,
(6) the promotion of the nonparticipants.

Involving the users of program evaluation information in the development process is not a panacea, but it helps (Patton, 1978). During my first year as a program evaluator, I inferred that our CMHC Outpatient Department staff would *"love"* goal attainment scaling, and that it would serve needs ranging from accountability and evaluation to quality assurance and continuing education. The Outpatient staff *did not* love goal attainment scaling. Quite to the contrary, it was fully two years before the fallout from that experience subsided and before evaluation was able to reenter that system of our CMHC. A subsequent attempt at assessing treatment outcome with input from an advisory board of *line staff* resulted in a far more tenable evaluation assessment technique, combining pragmatic issues with the commitment of staff within each department to follow through with the evaluation.

To enhance the usability of data base information, whether computerized or manual, *spend time* first with the people who are going to make decisions and policy based on the data, find out the kinds of information they *need,* the information they *want,* and with what frequency they need to receive the information.

NEEDS ASSESSMENT

Assessment of service needs is a neglected and misunderstood aspect of human service program planning. Optimally, legislative blueprints for national social and health programs should emerge from systematic, scientific need assessment efforts that are designed to identify the extent and degree of need for specific services in the general population. In practice, however, national programs emerge from a political context of confrontation between special and general interests, social service ideologies, demands for service, and the competition for access to resources.

As a result, our communities are peppered with uncoordinated and loosely integrated programs that overlap and compete for sparse resources. Without adequate assessment of human service needs, this poorly monitored and uncoordinated situation will persist and worsen [Siegel et al., 1978:215].

While the service elements of the CMHC program traditionally have been structured, there remained the flexibility for local centers to develop priorities based on community *needs* and existing *resources*. A justification, or needs assessment, is required in the initial grant applications for a CMHC. In 1974, however, a special report to Congress had these comments about CMHC planning and needs assessment:

A better job needs to be done in identifying local mental health needs. . . . Most centers reviewed had not made specific studies of their catchment areas which would enable them to set priorities and compare services provided against these priorities.

The availability of funds to match Federal grants and the interests of the professional staffs of the centers were often important influences in establishing program emphasis within a center.

Although needs met by programs established in this manner are probably valid, there is no assurance that they are the only needs or the highest priority needs of the catchment areas. Also, once programs are established, they tend to dominate center activities in subsequent years.

Citizen participation and community involvement in center programs has varied widely, ranging from minimal to active. Community representatives and advisory groups have often had little voice in setting program priorities and direction or in determining how center funds are to be used [U.S. General Accounting Office, 1974:ii].

Additionally, a recent and critical perspective of the needs assessment process is offered in a report from the Assistant Secretary for Planning and Evaluation of the Department of Health, Education and Welfare (1977). While the report emphasizes that needs assessment requirements play a major role in federal grant-in-aid mechanisms, not a single program definition of needs assessment could be found in 36 major program areas. The author of this report, Wayne Kimmel, goes on to state:

> Most human resources agency heads, for example, probably have "control" (only indirect) over no more than about five per cent of their agency's budget. The rest is *already committed* to ongoing programs with built in growth factors and purposes specified in statutes [U.S. Dept. of Health, Education and Welfare, 1977:55].

Hence, the greatest pitfall for the utilization of needs assessment information is: Without the flexibility to make policy or programmatic changes suggested by the information, expectations are likely to be artificially raised and evaluation resources ineffectively used. The impact of needs assessment efforts are *most* enhanced when programs are in their formative stages and when program priorities can be assigned without prior modifications of human and economic resources.

COST ACCOUNTING

Needs assessment is conducted to assure responsiveness and accountability in program planning and development. Cost accounting is another accountability mechanism, often partially transferred into the responsibilities of program evaluation departments. As disenchantment with the programs of the "Great Society" and a declining economy intersected, human service programs saw the end of the free lunch from bottomless government coffers. The CMHC program was no exception. As decreasing federal dollars have meant more emphasis on cost containment in the CMHC programs, so too have program evaluators become concerned with the *cost* of programs as well as their *outcomes* (Carter and Newman, 1976; Fishman, 1975; Smith and Sorensen, 1974; Sorensen and Grove, 1978). However, these are the competencies that are perhaps *most* lacking in program evaluators at the agency level. In an age of increasing federal participation in health care financing, impending national health insurance, and "already here" Proposition 13, the importance of this evaluation category on the development of future agency policy will no doubt rapidly increase.

For the most part, however, present agency evaluators are still largely ill-prepared for the task of integrating the *outcomes* and the assessment of programs on clients with the measurement of the level of service required in *economic* terms. These skills appear to be easily acquired, nonetheless, and the linkages of costs and outcomes should clearly carry more weight with program directors and governing board members than mere descriptions of quantity of services and general statements about therapeutic outcome. While evaluators and clinicians are frequently concerned with monitoring the outcome of therapeutic interventions, the *costs* of services are often the most sensitive issue when making evaluation findings public. Program directors even of demonstrably effective services are hesitant to acknowledge high associated costs. Evaluators can, however, anticipate this sensitivity to fiscal issues and do some advance planning.

This brings us to our second theme, which borrows from the futurists and becomes a concept I call *"a surprise-free evaluation."* Even the most sophisticated evaluation request can, early in the process, be addressed by the evaluator with "I can tell you *right now* what we're going to find: (If the evaluation is summative in nature), the findings will either (1) *support* the program's goal attainment, (2) *refute it,* or (3) produce *equivocal findings."*

Role responsibilities and expectations between evaluator and decision maker, and the purposes to which the study will be used regardless of outcome, need to be *formalized in advance* to assure the utilization of the study. A number of authors have even suggested a *written evaluation contract* between the parties as helpful in this process.

A local evaluator can ask the project director what actions are possible under each of the three possible conditions. For example: Comparing the cost outcome of a cohort of patients in a CMHC's *day hospital* program versus *inpatient facility* may indicate that certain patients would make better clinical progress at less cost in the day hospital. But if the loss of the considerably higher inpatient revenue from this kind of treatment means the program director cannot take positive action, an evaluation focused on this specific question may have little influence on policy. The obligations of the evaluator, if any, to pursue an area also need to be explored in advance (Windle and Neigher, 1978)

There should, in fact, be relatively *few surprises* in the findings of evaluation studies; if one knows in advance that a certain range of likely or expected evaluation results back decision makers into untenable positions, evaluation is likely to produce little impact upon policy.

Obviously, this is an oversimplification and not a suggestion for an "'all or none'' decision-making process about when to proceed with an evaluation. Rather, it seems that a great deal can be done to enhance the impact of the evaluation *before* the process begins.

Patton's earlier quotation that ends with "But it doesn't tell us anything we really want to know" has a particularly haunting quality. I have proceeded at great length and with great intensity in evaluation projects for which I thought we all knew exactly what we wanted to know. Patton (1978) cites a parable:

> Nasrudin used to take his donkey across a frontier every day, with the cart loaded with straw. Since he admitted to being a smuggler when he trudged home every night, the frontier guards searched him again and again. They searched his person, sifted the straw, steeped it in water, even burned it from time to time. Meanwhile he was becoming visibly more and more prosperous.
>
> Then he retired and went to live in another country. Here one of the customs officers met him years later.
>
> "You can tell me now, Nasrudin," he said. "Whatever was it that you were smuggling, when we could never catch you at?"
>
> "Donkeys," said Nasrudin [Shaw, 1964: 59].

A second example is a more personal one and relates to our first theme about role clarification.

For a number of years I was involved in a program called the Primary Prevention Project, aimed at the early identification and intervention with children at psychological risk in the early primary grades. A promise was made not to ask for classroom teacher cooperation for the next school year unless the program was demonstrably effective. After two years of a "true" experiment, multiple regression and analyis of covariance data indicated there was *no statistical evidence* to support the contention that our program had a substantive and reliable impact on children in the program compared to matched controls. Fearing that the evaluation design was not as comprehensive as possible and that misunderstanding of the data by a lay school board would prematurely jeopardize the program's funding and *future viability*, I was obsessed during August about what to do with the data, as September and the new school year rapidly approach. To all of our amazement, we learned suddenly one evening that the school board refunded the program, based *solely on the additional number of children* carried on child study team roles. In fact, a summative evaluation of program effectiveness reflected *my values* of what the school board *should* want, rather than the simply *formative types* of information they actually used on which to base their refunding decision.

Even more importantly, there is an *ethical conflict* between the evaluation role of *advocacy* and that of *accountability*. I started out with an *accountability model,* promising full disclosure of program effectiveness to the local school board. After I saw the data, however, I shifted to an *advocacy model* out of the admittedly pretentious and self-serving notion that the program was indeed valuable, that my data could not correctly be interpreted by a lay board, and that I was the person to make those decisions. An evaluator may certainly play more than one role or apply several models; shifts out of convenience or self-interest are *"unkosher"* at best and *unethical* at worst.

While we often recognize the values and inconsistent role demands in the evaluation process, we *rarely* challenge the assumptions and values inherent in our methodological paradigms. As Patton (1978: 203) concludes:

> Evaluation research is dominated by the largely unquestioned, natural science paradigm of hypothetico-deductive methodology.

This dominant paradigm assumes quantitative measurement, experimental design, and multivariate, parametric statistical analysis to be the epitome of "good" science.

The balance between validily and relevance is not easily achieved in human service settings such as a CMHC. Without the resources of a university and the support group of other "like-minded" evaluators, we rely on the familiar, usually "experimental" roots of our training. For example, all of us have read Campbell and Stanley (1969) and are familiar with many alternatives to traditional experimental designs. I suspect, however, that many of us are still seduced by a "true" experiment and sophisticated methodology. After a particularly intense hand-wringing session, as NIMH's Chuck Windle listened patiently to me bemoan my .06 level of significance in one evaluation effort between program participants and nonparticipants, he offered the following: "Just because it isn't *publishable* doesn't mean it's not *actionable*."

Whatever the evaluation design, we must recognize, as Berk and Rossi (1976) suggest, that our most "empirical" approaches are full of moral and political value judgments. There are good examples in the recent literature of strategies for evaluators to synthesize the competing demands of science politics. For example, Berk (1977) offers a contextual schema to consider both methodology and policy. Additionally, goals clarification "technologies" such as Edwards' (1965) "Multiattribute-utility measurement" decision theory approach does much for placing values up front and getting all of the players into the game early.

Whatever positive actions we have taken so far in clearly specifying *evaluation roles*, identification of *appropriate decision makers* and information users, and clearly defining the evaluation *process and goal,* we still must communicate what happens to those who asked for the evaluation in the first place. At our worst we elaborate, enumerate, and obfuscate in our own self-interest or, as Moynihan (1969) suggests, social scientists are guilty of at least aiding and abetting "maximum feasible misunderstanding." Carol Weiss stated she longs to meet a one-armed program evaluator, someone who will not walk into her office with the final project report and reply to "What happened?" with "Well, on the one hand . . ., but on the other hand. . . ." The impact of evaluation on policy is enhanced when the evaluation reports concentrate on *decisions* rather than *conclusions,* on *applications* rather than *implications,* and on *utilization* rather than *replication.*

CONCLUSIONS

Finally, several additional factors seem essential to maximizing evaluation for planned change.

One is *a "personal" factor.* Illustrating from Patton's study of 20 HEW health evaluation systems:

> [Where] some individual takes direct, personal responsibility for getting the information to the right people, evaluations have an impact. Where the personal factor is *absent,* there is a marked absence of impact. Utilization is not simply determined by some configuration of abstract factors; it is determined in large part by real live caring human beings [Patton, 1978:69].

This finding is supported by other empirical investigations and by what we all really know.

The second factor is that evaluation works in a *political context.* We ought to be able to anticipate sooner than we do the likely utilization of evaluation data within our organizations. Count your votes and pick your projects. As Fairweather and his colleagues suggest, "Learn to lose gracefully (Fairweather et al., 1974:195).

We probably can do more to help our own cause at the agency level by being *proactive,* rather than *retroactive,* in exploring evaluation outcomes and decision alternatives. Finally, we may need to adopt more *realistic expectation* for the impact of our work, as Patton suggests:

> We found in interviews with federal decisionmakers that evaluation research is used by decisionmakers, but not in the clearcut,

organization-shaking ways in which social scientists sometimes believe research should be used. Our data suggest that what is typically characterized as underutilization or nonutilization of evaluation reserach can be attributed in substantial degree to a narrow definition of utilization that fails to take into consideration the nature of actual decisionmaking processes in most programs. Utilization of research findings is not something that suddenly and concretely occurs at some one distinct moment in time. Rather, utilization is a diffuse and gradual process of reducing decisionmaker uncertainty within an existing social context [Patton, 1978:34].

When particular social context is federally associated mental health care, the decision process is *already* full of uncertainties: changing "essential" services in federal legislation (PI 88164; 91211; 9463), shifting local service priorities, and dwindling federal funds with few new revenue sources to replace them. The complex organizational structure of many CHMCs makes the challenge even greater, especially when program managers are clinicians rather than professional administrators.

It would seem, then, that the underutilization of program evaluation in the mental health care programs is more than a cause for academic discourse. Its opportunities for impact are evidently there, just as are its opportunities for falling short of expectations. CMHCs did not spontaneously develop evaluation capabilities out of internally felt needs—in fact, evaluation for "self-improvement" was more or less forced upon them by legislation. We have tried in this chapter to present the view that evaluation means different things to different people involved in mental health services. It may turn out, as Windle (1976) warns, that evaluation is an "embarrassment of opportunity," not being the expected cure-all for wasteful or ineffective mental health programs. At the same time, though, we see steps that evaluators can take in these settings to create *realistic*, a priori expectations about this craft and its usefulness.

REFERENCES

ATTIKISSON, C. C., and T. D. NGUYEN (1978) "Contributions of evaluation research to mental health service delivery policy." Presented at the 86th Annual Meeting of the American Psychological Association, Toronto, Canada, August.

ATTKISSON, C. C., T. R. BROWN, and W. A. HARGREAVES (1978a) "Roles and functions of evaluation in human service programs." In C. C. Attkisson, W. A. Hargreaves, M.J. Horowitz, and J.E. Sorensen (eds.) Evaluation of Human Service Programs. New York: Academic Press.

ATTKISSON, C. C., W. A. HARGREAVES, M.J. HOROWITZ, and J. E. SORENSON [eds.] (1978b) Evaluation of Human Service Programs. New York: Academic Press.

BERK, R. A. (1977) "Discretionary methodological decisions in applied research." Sociological Methods and Research 5: 317-334.

BERK, R. A. and P. H. ROSSI (1976) "Doing good or worse: evaluation research politically re-examined." Social Problems 337-349.

BLOOM, B. L. (1977) Community Mental Health: A General Introduction. Monterey, CA:Brooks/Cole.

CAMPBELL, D. (1969) "Reforms as experiments." American Psychologist 24: 409-429.

CAMPBELL, D. and J. STANLEY (1969) Experimental and Quasi-Experimental Designs for Research. Chicago: Rand McNally.

CARTER, D. E. and F. L. NEWMAN (1976) A Client-Oriented System of Mental Health Service Delivery and Program Management: A Workbook and Guide. (DHEW Publication No. ADM-76-307.) Washington, DC: U.S. Government Printing Office.

CHAPMAN, R. L. (1976) The Design of Management Information Systems for Mental Health Organizations: A Primer. (DHEW Publication No. ADM 76-333). Washington, DC: U.S. Government Printing Office.

DAVIS, H. R. and S. E. SALASIN (1975) "The utilization of evaluation." In E. L. Struening, and M. Guttentag (eds.) Handbook of Evaluation Research (Vol. 1). Beverly Hills, CA: Sage.

EDWARDS, W. (1965) "Tactical notes on the relation between scientific and statistical hypothesis." Psychological Bulletin 63(6).

FISHMAN, D. B. (1975) "Development of a generic cost-effectiveness methodology for evaluating the patient services of a community mental health center." In J. Zusman and C. R. Wurster (eds.), Program Evaluation: Alcohol, Drug Abuse, and Mental Health Services. Lexington, MA: D.C. Heath.

FAIRWEATHER, G. W., D. H. SANDERS, and L. G. TORNATZKY (1974) Creating Change in Mental Health Organizations. New York: Pergamon.

LANDSRERG, G., R. HAMMER, and W. NEIGHER (1978) "Analyzing the evaluation activities in CMHC's in NIMH Region II." Presented at the 1978 Annual Meeting of the National Council of Community Mental Health Centers, Kansas City, Missouri, February.

LANDSBERG, G. W. D. NEIGHER, R. J. HAMMER, C. WINDLE, and J. R. WOY [eds.] (1979) Evaluation in Practice, A Sourcebook of Program Evaluation Studies from Mental Care Systems in the United States (DHEW Publication No. ADM 78-763.) Washington, DC: U.S. Government Printing Office.

MOYNIHAN, D. P. (1969) Maximum Feasible Misunderstanding. New York: Free Press.

NEIGHER, W. D. (1979) "Evaluation perspectives matrix." In G. Landsberg, W. D. Neigher, R.J. Hammer, C. Windle, and J.R. Woy (eds.) Evaluation in Practice. A Sourcebook of Program Evaluation Studies from Mental Health Care Systems in the United States (DHEW Publication No. ADM 78-763). Washington, DC: U.S. Government Printing Office.

National Institute of Mental Health (1977) "Guidelines for program evaluation." (working draft)

National Institute of Mental Health (1978) Provisional Data on Federally Funded Community Mental Health Centers, 1976-1977. Prepared by Survey and Reports Branch, Division of Biometry and Epidemiology, May.

PATTON, M. Q. (1978) Utilization-Focused Evaluation. Beverly Hills, CA: Sage.

ROSSI, P. H. (1978) "Issues in the evaluation of human services delivery." Evaluation Quarterly 2:573-599.

SIEGEL, L. M., C. C. ATTKISSON, and L. G. CARSON (1978) "Need identification and program planning in the community context." In C.C. Attkisson, W.A. Hargreaves, M.J. Horowitz, and J.E. Sorensen (eds.) Evaluation of Human Service Programs. New York: Academic Press.

SHAW, I. The Sufis. New York: Doubleday.

SMITH, T. and J. SORENSEN (1974) Integrated Management Information Systems for Community Mental Health Centers (DHEW Publication No. ADM 75-165). Washington, DC: U.S. Government Printing Office.

SORENSEN, J. E. and H. D. GROVE (1978) "Using cost-outcome and cost-effectiveness analyses for improved program management and accountability." In C.C. Attkisson, W.A. Hargreaves, M.J. Horowitz, and J.E. Sorensen (eds.) Evaluation of Human Service Program. New York: Academic Press.

U.S. Department of Health, Education and Welfare (1977) Needs Assessment: A Critical Perspective. Prepared by Wayne A. Kimmel for Office of the Assistant Secretary for Planning and Evaluation, December. Washington, DC: U.S. Government Printing Office.

U.S. General Accounting Office (1974) "Need for more effective management of Community Mental Health Center's program." Report to the Congress, B-164032(5), Washington, D.C.: U.S. Government Printing Office.

WINDLE, C. (1976) "A crisis for program evaluation: an embarrassment of opportunity." Rhode Island Medical Journal (November):503, 504, 510, 516.

WINDLE, C. and W. D. NEIGHER (1978) "Ethical problems in program evaluation: advice for trapped evaluators." Evaluation and Program Planning 1:97-107.

PART IV

Planning for Policy-Oriented Evaluations:
The Third World Experience

8

Elliott R. Morss
Development Alternatives, Inc.

MONITORING AND EVALUATING
RURAL DEVELOPMENT PROJECTS
Barriers to the Utilization of Information Systems

> *"The word 'system' in the term 'information system' is troubling. It implies logic, order, rationality, formality and great expense. I don't give a damn about any of these. In fact, I don't give a damn about information. I just want to make the right decisions."*
> —*Quote from an Anonymous Project Manager, 1977.*

In recent years there has been growing recognition of the importance of equipping rural development projects with information systems to monitor and evaluate activities. Development Alternatives, Inc. (DAI) has spent considerable time in both the conceptual development of such systems and attempts to introduce them into rural development projects. In retrospect, we are not ecstatic about what we have been able to accomplish in our earlier work,[1] although experience may be paying off in more recent endeavors (see Weisel, 1978). Robert Levine, former head of the U.S. Office of Economic Opportunity, suggests that we are not alone:

> Time and time again, Federal agencies at the top have tried to impose nationwide data systems; they have always failed [Levine, 1972: 149].

Clearly, the problems of making an information system in a rural development project work differ from those of a national-level system; however, in both instances, it is worth pausing to reflect upon the barriers to utilization.

In our work, we have found:

- Very few effective information systems in operation that are inexpensive enough to permit extensive replication; and
- that while there are serious methodological problems, they are not the only or the primary reasons for the dearth of information systems in use.

The purpose of this chapter is to summarize our findings on barriers to the utilization of monitoring/evaluation systems. While similar utilization problems exist for sector, national, and international systems, we will focus on the utilization problems of project managers.[2]

THE POTENTIALS FOR PROJECT MONITORING/EVALUATION SYSTEMS

Ideally, project monitoring/evaluation systems should (1) track inputs and outputs against schedules; (2) measure project effects (impacts); (3) identify current and upcoming problems; (4) diagnose reasons for problems; and (5) prescribe project solutions. Our discussion of these items is selective and short on the grounds that the problems have more to do with the realization of these potentials than with their specification. Little needs to be said about the first item; the need to track inputs and outputs is recognized, and most projects have systems that accomplish this task to a greater or lesser extent.

Over the last decade, it has been recognized that the timely achievement of project outputs (for example, the completion of roads, bridges, and buildings) does not ensure the attainment of project goals (that is, output achievements are not proxies for goal attainments). This realization, coupled with new foreign assistance directives to focus benefits on the rural poor, has necessitated efforts to measure project effects directly. Considerable creativity is required for the design of an information system to measure significant project effects at reasonable cost.

To be of greatest use, a project monitoring/evaluation system should go beyond the measurement of project effects. It should also be capable of identifying upcoming problems; diagnosing the reasons for them; and generating information that leads to their resolution through project modifications, project redesign, and attempts at project replications elsewhere.

Clearly, getting an information system to deliver on all of the potentials spelled out above is a tall order. The starting point of this chapter is the observation that very few projects have information systems that even begin to realize these potentials.[3] Our purpose is to give our ideas about why this is so.

Why Systems Are Not Utilized

Clearly, there is much work yet to be done on information utilization in rural development projects. The purpose of this section is to summarize our experience and findings in the literature[4] on why projects make little use of monitoring and evaluation systems.

THREAT TO PROJECT MANAGEMENT

It would be naive to ignore the fact that formal monitoring and evaluation acticities can be seen as a threat by project managers. The situation is clearly depicted in the following quote from an expert on information utilization:

> Organizations invariably respond to factors other than the attainment of their formal goals. Even rudimentary knowledge of organizational behavior indicates the salience of the drive for organizational perpetuation, personnel's needs for status and esteem and their attachment to the practice skills in which they have invested a professional lifetime, conservatism and inertia and fear of the unknown consequences of change, sensitivity to the reactions of various publics, costs, prevailing ideological doctrines, political feasibility, and the host of other considerations that affect the maintenance of the organization. Evaluation's evidence of program outcome cannot override all the other contending influences.

A fascinating example of resistance to utilization can be borrowed from military history. In 1940-41 the RAF Bomber Command refused to accept the evidence of aerial photography on the failure of its missions. Photographs indicated that only one of every four aircraft reporting an attack on target had actually gotten within five miles of it. An officer who passed on to his chief an interpretation showing that an attack had missed its mark found it later on his desk with a note scrawled across it in red: "I do not accept this report." The author of the account of these events states, in words that will echo familiarly to social evaluators, "it was very natural that many of those whose work it affected jumped to the comforting conclusion that something must have been wrong with the camera or the photographs or the man who wrote the report [Weiss, 1972: 319-320].

To a greater or lesser extent, formal project information systems will threaten project management. The threat will be greater if the information system emphasizes summative evaluation rather than problem identification and resolution.

MANAGEMENT INABILITY TO ANTICIPATE INFORMATION NEEDS

It appears that project managers and other key project policy makers find it difficult to specify in advance what information they need to monitor and evaluate project activities. This task then falls to so-called "information experts," who then take it upon themselves to construct the information systems.

This is frequently the beginning of the end; the information specialists design the system in a vacuum and it becomes irrelevant from the standpoint of potential users' perceived needs.

EXCESSIVE COST

Frequently, an expert is hired to design a project information system. The expert is often paid for completing an information system design, but not for system execution. Under these circumstances, it is not surprising that information system designs often err on the side of being too complex and costly to be implemented (for example, for five person-weeks of work, it is "safer" to submit a 30-page data collection document than a one-page document, even if the latter is more appropriate in light of available project resources).

Frequently, information system designs are far more complex and costly than warranted for another reason. Insufficient attention has been given to limiting the information to be collected and analyzed to what is critical for anticipated policy needs. It is far easier to require information "related to policy issues" than to require information "relevant to policy decisions." Granted, not all information needs can be anticipated; however, cost considerations suggest that information collection should be limited to information needs as expressed by project managers.

RELEVANT DATA ARE TOO EXPENSIVE

Much work remains to be done on low-cost data collection and analysis techniques, and it remains a strong possibility that even the costs of collection and analysis of relevant data will "break the bank." There is clearly some upper limit on the amount project funders will pay for information systems. The implication of this haunting thought is that several of the potentials of information systems mentioned earlier will have to be given up on the grounds that they are too expensive to realize.

A few comments are in order concerning the way that information costs are measured. Only the marginal or extra costs resulting from the information system should be included in the accounting of information system costs. An information system will be much less expensive if it draws on the information the project staff would acquire in carrying out its normal activities than if a new system is superimposed on existing work. It is also important to attribute costs to the potential users. A project should not be saddled with the costs, in either accounting or monetary terms, of information that will benefit only an external donor or a national ministry. More work on the proper measurement and allocation of information system costs is needed.

TIMING

Evaluations frequently are not used because the results do not come in until after the policy decision for which the evaluation was undertaken has been made. The scenario unfolds as follows: Policy makers, unable to anticipate their information needs in advance, commission evaluations at the last minute. The evaluation designs do not take into account the policy makers' time constraints. The resulting activity is then a waste.

RECOMMENDATIONS THAT CANNOT BE USED

The tale is often told of a problem Coca-Cola encountered many years ago when the vending machine price had to be raised from five cents because of inflation. After a lengthy and expensive study of the problem, a consulting firm came in with the recommendation to increase the vending price for a bottle of Coke to seven and one-half cents.

Evaluations are sometimes not used because the recommendations are beyond the power of policy makers to implement. Recommendations are not followed at times because they are not compatible with the constraints and/or other objectives of policy makers. Finally, recommendations are not used because they are either not understood or not trusted by policy makers.

RIGID PROJECT DESIGN

If project funds must be spent in a predetermined way, there is no point in investing resources in a monitoring and evaluation system that tells how to redesign the project to improve project performance. While such inflexible project designs do exist, we doubt that such rigidities would stand up to solid documentation, provided by a good monitoring/evaluation system, that changes are needed.

ROOT CAUSES OF NONUSE AND REMEDIES

The reasons that information systems are not used stem from either or both of two primary causes:

(1) Project management has insufficient appreciation of the potentials of a monitoring/evaluation system; and/or
(2) the system design does not reflect the needs of and/or constraints under which the project operates.

Our experience and the information utilization literature provided thorough documentation that policy makers (read project managers) cannot anticipate their information needs; and that policy makers are oriented to solving current problems and can rarely sustain an interest in the design of an information system. Consequently, the information system design is turned over to information specialists. The information management literature suggests that information specialists: (1) have trouble distinguishing between relevant and "related to" data; (2) spend more time than they should conceptualizing rather than customizing information systems for specific applications; (3) give too little time to the cost dimension of establishing and maintaining information systems; and (4) are biased toward formal information systems.

The following tentative recommendations are offered in concluding this chapter:

(1) Increase the ratio of customizing to conceptualizing time.
(2) Build the information system into the project design so that project management has the responsibility to deliver on this mandate from the outset.
(3) Don't try to introduce an information system into an ongoing project unless project management is thoroughly involved as well as interested in making the system useful to the project.
(4) Where various information systems are already in place in the project area, try to rationalize them to your needs rather than create a new and perhaps redundant system.

APPENDIX A
Information System Activities
of Development Alternatives, Inc.

Project	DAI Involvement
Paraguay Small Farmer Survey October 1973-October 1974	Methodological test of five different data collection techniques.
	Design of an analysis system for a small farmer computerized input/ourput and co-operative participation survey.

Thailand, Impact Assessment Evaluation December 1973

Review and evaluation of the Impact Assessment Information System within the Accelerated Rural Development Project.

Bolivia, Impact Assessment Design October 1973-1974

Three visits to the National Community Development Service participating in the design and field-testing of an indicator system for project impact.

Peru, Design for a Comprehensive Information System in the ORDEZA Project November 1973-December 1974

Six visits to design, test, and redesign more than a dozen different collection instruments covering all phases of a regional income-generating community development project.

Kenya, Information to Support a District Development Program 1974-1975

Full-time staff member working on small farmer questionnaires in the Vihiga Project.

Chile, Farm Records and Technical Assistance for Land Reform Farmers 1975-1978

Eight visits to design a detailed set of farm records, which are integrated into technical assistance to be provided by the private sector.

Kenya, Support to the District Development Program Within the Ministry of Finance and Planning 1975-1976

A full-time staff member to create an information system appropriate to the needs of district development in Kenya.

Tanzania, Support to the Hanang Rural Health Project 1977-1978

Three visits to assist in the design and implementation of a comprehensive information system project.

Kenya, Support to the Kitui Rural Health Project 1977-1978

One visit completed and more scheduled to assist in the design and implementation of a comprehensive information system.

Zaire, Support to the North Shaba Integrated Rural Development Project 1978, ongoing

The design of a comprehensive information system in a large rural development project.

Reports and Publications

Donald R. Mickelwait, "Information Systems to Support Rural Development Project," in Elliott R. Morss, John K. Hatch, Donald R. Mickelwait, Charles F. Sweet, *Strategies for Small Farmer Development.* Boulder, CO: Westview Press, 1976.

Donald R. Mickelwait and Alan Roth, "A Short Paper on Information Collection and Analysis To Support Agricultural and Rural Development Projects." DAI Occasional Staff Paper, revised February 3, 1977.

Peter F. Weisel, "Monitoring and Evaluating Rural Development Programmes with Specific Reference to the Integrated Agricultural Development Programme." Ministry of Finance and Planning, Kenya, March 1977.

Peter F. Weisel and R. W. Machina, "District Planning: Proposals for Local Level Planning and Management." Ministry of Finance and Planning, Kenya, March 1977.

Donald R. Mickelwait, Alan Roth, and George Poynor, "Information for Decision-making in Rural Development." Draft report for the Agency for International Development, April 1977 (under revision).

Elliott R. Morss et al., "Final Report of the Value Burden Study Group" to the Federal Paperwork Commission, February 1977.

Peter F. Weisel, "Information Systems for Project Management and Evaluation: A Case Study in Northern Tanzania," March 1978.

Elliott R. Morss, "Barriers to the Utilization of Information Systems to Monitor and Evaluate Rural Development Projects." Prepared for the OECD Seminar on Monitoring/Evaluation of Rural Development Projects, March 1978.

APPENDIX B
Sample Bibliography on Information Utilization Research

Books

Caplan, N. and Barton, E. *Social Indicators '73: A Study of the Relationship Between the Power of Information and Utilization by Federal Executives.* Institute for Social Research, University of Michigan, 1976.

Caplan, N., Morrison, A., and Stambaugh, R. J. *The Use of Social Science Knowledge in Policy Decisions at the National Level.* Ann Arbor: Institute for Social Research, University of Michigan, 1971.

Horowitz, Irving L. (ed.) *The Use and Abuse of Social Science: Behavioral Science and National Policy-Making.* New Brunswick, NJ: Transaction Books, 1971.

National Institute of Mental Health. *Planning for Creative Change in Mental Health Services: A Distillation of Principles on Research Utilization.* Washington, DC: U.S. Government Printing Office, DHEW Publication Nos. (HSM) 71-9060 and 9061, 1971.

Sackman, Y. and Nie, Norman (eds.) *The Information Utility of Social Choice.* Montvale, NJ: AFIPS Press, 1970. (especially Eulau article.)

Weiss, Carol H., *Improving the Linkage Between Social Research and Public Policy,* Bureau of Applied Social Research, Columbia University, August 1975.

Periodicals

Freeman, James E. and Rubenstein, Albert H. The Users and Uses of Scientific and Technical Information: Critical Research Needs, *Research Institute,* 52 pp., November 1974.

Kitsuse, John and Cicourel, Aaron V. "A Note on the Use of Official Statistics," *Social Problems,* 1969, 11, 131-139.

Larsen, Judith "Dissemination and Utilization of Information." Progress Report, October 1-31, NIMH Grant No. MH-25121. Palo Alto, CA: American Institutes for Research, 1974.

Larsen, Judith "Diffusion of Innovations Among Community Mental Health Centers." Progress Report, December 1-31. Palo Alto, CA: American Institutes for Research, 1973.

Lund, Sander "A Measure of Organizational Readiness to Adopt Program Evaluation Technology." *Program Evaluation Resources Center,* 1974.

Mayer, Steven E. "Are you Ready to Accept Program Evaluation?," *P.E.R.C. Newsletter,* 1975 IV (January-February).

Roos, Noralou P. "Influencing the Health Care System: Policy alternatives." *Public Policy,* 1974, 22, 139-167.

Other Sources

Lobb, Judith and Ciarlo, James A. "Predicted Relative Utilization of Community Mental Health Center in the City and County of Denver." Unpublished Manuscript, Mental Health Systems Evaluation Project, University of Denver, Colorado, 1975.

Rossman, Betty "The Impact of Program Evaluation on Decision Making in a Community Mental Health Center." Unpublished manuscript, Mental Health Systems Evaluation Project, University of Denver, Colorado, 1975.

Use of Social Research in Federal Domestic Programs: A Staff Study for the Research and Technical Programs Sub-Committee of the Committee on Government Operations, House of Representatives, April 1967 (Vols. 2 and 3). Washington, DC: U.S. Government Printing Office.

NOTES

1. See Appendix A for a listing of DAI's information systems activities.

2. Project information also can be useful to project participants. Getting small farmers to use project information involves a set of problems that will not be discussed in this chapter.

3. This comment refers to information systems that are inexpensive enough to replicate on a large scale. There are some expensive "research" projects that have realized most of these potentials.

4. It should be noted that a considerable amount of research has been done on the utilization of information (see Appendix B for a sample). Unfortunately, very little research has been done on this question in the context of rural development projects.

REFERENCES

LEVINE, R. A. (1972) Public Planning. New York: Basic Books.

WEISEL, P. F. (1978) "Information systems for project management and evaluation: a case study in Northern Tanzania." March.

WEISS, C. H. (1972) "Utilization of evaluation: toward comparative study." In C. H. Weiss (ed.), Evaluating Action Programs: Readings in Social Action and Education. Boston: Allyn & Bacon.

ABOUT THE CONTRIBUTORS

DR. ANDRE L. DELBECQ is the Dean of the Graduate School of Business at the University of Santa Clara. Prior to 1979, he was on the faculty of the Graduate School of Business and the School of Social Work at the University of Wisconsin for 12 years. He is a Fellow of the Academy of Management and has published extensively in program planning, evaluation, and management.

EUGENIE WALSH FLAHERTY is the Director of Research and Evaluation for the Philadelphia Health Management Corporation. She received her doctorate in Experimental Psychology, with a secondary emphasis in the history and philosophy of psychology, from the New School of Social Research in 1973. Her interests are in the development of the field of evaluation, drug abuse, mental health legislation, and adolescent family planning.

SANDRA L. GILL is a doctoral candidate in Program Design: Evaluation at the University of Wisconsin-Madison. She has been a management consultant since 1974 and spent five years in state and federal human service administration prior to her doctoral studies.

DR. H. DURWARD HOFLER is Assistant Professor of Business and Management at Northeastern Illinois University, teaches courses on Research and on The Management of Change at the Traffic Institute of Northwestern University, and is President of Systems Facilitation Associates, Inc. He has been Director of Human Resources in a large U.S. corporation, Research Associate with the Center for the Interdisciplinary Study of Science and Technology of Northwestern University, and consultant for private and government organizations. He has co-authored numerous policy and research analyses for government agencies in the area of innovation and program development. He has a B.A. from Duke University and a Ph.D. from Northwestern University.

ANN MAJCHRZAK is currently working on her Ph.D. dissertation at the Department of Psychology at UCLA. Her research interests primarily focus on an organizational perspective to the performance and utilization of program evaluation. Specializing in social service and mental health programs, Ann consults with community-based programs to aid in their program evaluation and development efforts.

ELLIOTT R. MORSS is Director of Research at Development Alternatives, Inc., a Washington-based consulting firm that works in the development field. Trained as an economist, Dr. Morss has taught at Harvard and the University of Michigan. In recent years, Dr. Morss' main interests have been bureaucratic dynamics, social indicators, and evaluation methodologies. He has just completed a book with Robert Rich on government information systems to be published this fall by Westview Press. His most recent book publication is *New Directions in Development: A Study of U.S. Aid* (written with Donald R. Mickelwait and Charles F. Sweet, Westview Press, 1979).

WILLIAM D. NEIGHER is Assistant Director of Saint Clare's Hospital Community Mental Health Center in Denville, New Jersey. He has been a consultant in mental health program evaluation and planning to federal and state agencies as well as other CMHCs. He received his B.A. from the University of Massachusetts and Ph.D. in Psychology from Yeshiva University. For the past several years Dr. Neigher has worked on state, NIMH, and USPHS projects developing training conferences and resource materials in program evaluation. A social-community psychologist, he has taught at Lehman College, City University of New York, and Rutgers University, and is an editor of *Emerging Developments in Mental Health Program Evaluation* (1977) and *Evaluation in Practice* (1979).

MICHAEL RADNOR is Professor of Organization Behavior at the Northwestern University Kellogg Graduate School of Management and Director of the Northwestern Center for the Interdisciplinary Study of Science and Technology. He received his undergraduate degree and diplomas from British schools and his doctorate in industrial engineering from Northwestern. Dr. Radnor has been principal investigator on several million dollars worth of research projects in the areas of innovation, R & D management, and policy-making, and is also a recognized authority in the organization and management of the management sciences and of operations research.

ROBERT F. RICH is Assistant Professor of Politics and Public Affairs at the Woodrow Wilson School of Public and International Affairs, Princeton University. He holds a Ph.D. in political science from the University of Chicago, has published extensively on the utilization of social research knowledge, and has served as a consultant for numerous evaluation design and research projects. Professor Rich currently is conducting a study of the determinants of mental health policy-making in the state of New Jersey. He is the author of the forthcoming book, *The Power of Social Science Information and Public Policy* (Jossey-Bass, 1979), and is the editor of a new journal, *Knowledge: Creation, Diffusion, Utilization,* published by Sage Publications.

JONAS WAIZER received his Ph.D. in psychology from the City University of New York and taught there and at Hofstra University. He is a founder and council member of the Eastern Evaluation Research Society. As the Acting Assistant Director of the New Jersey Division of Mental Health and Hospitals, he has responsibility for directing research, evaluation, and information systems development in an active collaboration of service provider agencies with federal, state, and county governments. Dr. Waizer's experiences in designing and implementing evaluation programs for mental health centers in New Jersey and New York have fueled an interest in the strategies for achieving its effective utilization by political decision makers. He is working on the design of a mental health management information system that can facilitate interagency accountability and evaluation in a unified human services system.

CHARLES WINDLE is Program Evaluation Specialist in the Mental Health Services Development Branch of the National Institute of Mental Health. His primary current interests include the development of methods for program evaluation, substantive evaluation of the Community Mental Health Centers Program, and citizen participation in mental health services planning and evaluation. Dr. Windle has a Ph.D. in experimental psychology from Columbia University and, before joining NIMH, worked for the Human Resources Research Organization, the Center for Research in Social Systems of American University, Pacific State Hospital in Pomona (California), and the Iranian Oil Exploration and Producing Company in Masjid-i-Sulaimon and Abadan (Iran).

J. RICHARD WOY is Acting Chief of the Program Analysis and Evaluation Branch, Office of Program Development and Analysis, National Institute of Mental Health. He holds a Ph.D. in clinical psychology from the University of Rochester. His primary current interests include evaluation, quality assurance and issues in the community-based care of the mentally ill. He has written a number of articles and chapters in these areas, his most recent publications including "Community Mental Health Centers and the Seed Money Concept: The Effects of Terminating Federal Funds" (with R. S. Weiner, S. S. Sharfstein, and R. D. Bass, in the *Community Mental Health Journal,* 1979) and *Evaluation in Practice: A Sourcebook of Program Evaluation Studies from Mental Health Care Systems in the United States* (co-edited with G. Landsberg, W. D. Neigher, R. J. Hammer, and C. Windle, GPO, 1979).